The Art Within Portrait Photography

A master photographer's revealing
and enlightening look at portraiture

by Klaus Bohn, MPA, F/SPPA, A

Feeling more deeply about photography

www.photographicartvictoria.com

Foreword by Ken Whitmire, M.Photog., CR, FASP

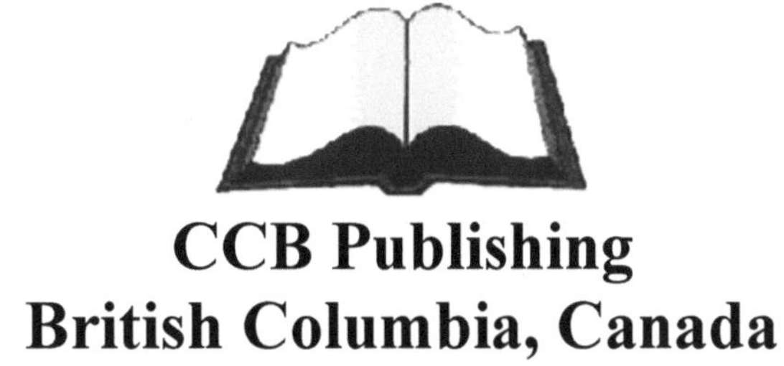

CCB Publishing
British Columbia, Canada

The Art Within Portrait Photography: A master photographer's revealing and enlightening look at portraiture

ISBN-10: 0-9781162-3-2
ISBN-13: 978-0-9781162-3-1
First Edition

Library and Archives Canada Cataloguing in Publication
Bohn, Klaus, 1945-
The art within portrait photography: a master photographer's revealing and enlightening look at portraiture / by Klaus Bohn; foreword by Ken Whitmire.
Includes index.
Also available in electronic format.
ISBN 978-0-9781162-3-1
1. Portrait photography. 2. Photography, Artistic. I. Title.
TR575.B57 2007 778.9'2 C2007-901364-3

Publisher: CCB Publishing
British Columbia, Canada
www.ccbpublishing.com

Dedication

I dedicate this book to my family and especially to my mother Elli Bohn as she is the one who we all go to during our time of need. My mother is a real Mom. You can talk to her about anything and everything, whatever may be on your mind. I remember as a very young child racing with her and at that time I would lose. She never gave me a cheap victory but there came a time when I could out run her and I know I can out run her now. There are things she will always be able to do that will out perform my efforts even to her dying day. She earns my respect each and every day as it streams from her charisma. I'm amazed how everyone, both young and old wants to hug her, even strangers. I don't know how she does it; it must be in her spirit!

To my mother who is so easy to LOVE.

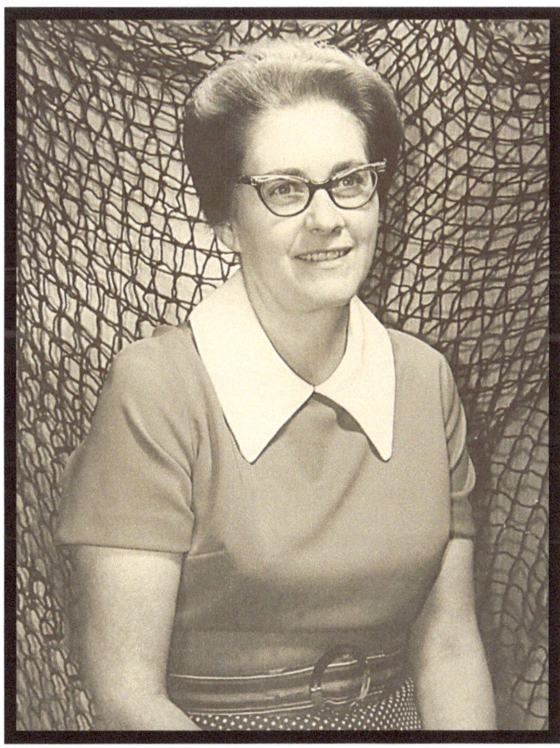

My Mom, circa 1972

Other books by Klaus Bohn

50 Principles of Composition in Photography

"Fantastic book!"
Clay Blackmore Photographer LLC

Giclee Prints by Klaus Bohn

Giclee prints of the images presented in this book
may be purchased directly through Klaus Bohn's web site:

www.photographicartvictoria.com

Foreword
by Ken Whitmire

Portraiture is described in most dictionaries as first, a likeness of a person, especially of the face as a painting, drawing, photograph, etc. and second, a verbal description usually, but not always, of a person. To portray is to represent by a drawing, painting, carving or in more modern times, the last 165 years, with the medium of photography.

Photography, the word, is of Greek derivation: photo meaning light and graph meaning drawn or written. The generally assumed definition is "drawing with light," "painting with light" or "portraying with light."

Photography ushered in a new era of recording images in that it records them optically, mechanically, chemically and/or electronically; much as the typewriter and subsequently the word processor changed the logistics of writing by mechanical and electronic means. Both the typewriter/word processor and the camera, of course, record exactly what is put into them. If anything creative, perceptive or otherwise worthwhile comes out of either, it must be placed there by the artist.

Just as there are precious few literary masterpieces produced on the average keyboard day in and day out, it follows that the recording of images in general, is just that: the camera records the likeness of what is put in front of it. The process of producing creative or perceptive manuscripts or images is pretty much the same as it has been for many hundreds of years. It must come from the minds of the artists.

We in the portrait photography profession are gradually coming to the realization that we have inherited this profession from the brush artists, painters and sculptors of a hundred or so years ago. It behoves us to occasionally stop and think, "What have we done with it?" Is our emphasis on *recording* or do we strive for portraits with essence, created and presented in a manner that first attracts the eye, and then makes a lasting impression on the mind?

It is portraitists like Klaus Bohn who have helped retain the artistic essence of the profession during the drastic logistical changes of the last couple of decades. Not only has Klaus produced a great body of portrait work, he has developed the talent to put into words the deeper meaning of his portraits: Why were they commissioned? What were they intended to accomplish? How did he arrive at his perceptions? and How did he logistically transfer these perceptions into reality "on the canvas," so to speak? Then finally, what mood or feeling did the finished portraits present to the viewers?; not only to the clients but to total strangers, who by just walking by become captivated by the essence and power of the presented imagery.

The Art Within Portrait Photography will not only be cherished by the general reader; for those in the profession of portraiture it is an added educational tool to gain knowledge and inspiration.

Ken Whitmire, M.Photog., CR, FASP

Contents

Introduction

Revealing the art within portrait photography allows us to create a greater awareness of ourselves and our surroundings. We often see photos of our families, loved ones, our treasured children, pets and so on but do we really see the emotions, feelings and art contained within these images? Many of us feel this overwhelming need to satisfy this craving to be the best we can be to our family and the families of the world. Likewise my approach has always been to fulfill this craving and be driven to explore the art and creativity that exists in portraiture as well as other forms of photography.

I have always been impressed with the talent of Gene Hattori and his great photography studio *F:11 Photographic Design* in Saskatoon. In many ways I looked up to him as one of my mentors. Gene ran a television commercial that included the words, "Who signs your portraits?" I was so impressed that a few years later I ran a similar ad on TV. There were images fading into one another with only music in the background until the very end when I spoke those same words, "Who signs your portraits?"

A valuable lesson was learned when I photographed a family who lived about an hour's drive from my studio. They made separate trips for their consultation, photographic session, projection and finally to pick up their wall portraits. Two hours after they left with their portraits I received a phone call from this client informing me that I had forgotten to sign their photographs! She said, "I will drive back tomorrow so that you can sign them." When counting each trip both ways that amounted to ten hours of travel. It was then that I realized in a profound way the value of a signature. How I treasured this family and was fortunate to photograph them many times over the years.

Another early impression on my career was made at a photographer's convention in Saskatchewan where Ken Whitmire was the main speaker. At that time I didn't know anything about him or his highly respected reputation but I have always remembered his images. They were very large with a generous use of space. One image still burned into my memory had a fireplace that extended all the way to the vaulted ceiling and the people were arranged with precision in the composition. Not only was I awe struck but a burning desire was created by this man to use space in a way that I had not seen before and I wanted to emulate Ken's vision. I fell in love with space. Another great artist who used space so effectively and also greatly influenced my vision was Thomas Gainsborough (1727-1788), an English painter of portraits, landscapes, and elegant pictures. He is considered one of the most individual geniuses in British art.

I lived most of my life in Saskatchewan with its big bright sky and lots of open spaces. Perhaps this has conditioned me to use lots of space. If we live in places that are crowded may we enjoy space in the artwork on our walls, freedom from claustrophobia; freedom from what sometimes feels like prison walls!

When studying another artist's work what impressions do we let soak in, what is our trigger factor? There are times we aim high but never pull the trigger or make it happen. We should all aim true and respond to our purpose, with dedication and commitment. I have been so fortunate to be in the company of many great photographers, study with them and read about their work and driving commitment. I had the privilege to hear Edward Weston's son speak and was moved by what he had to say about his father. I feel honoured to own a student print of his *Pepper No. 40* and look at it every day with appreciation for a true pioneer. D.H. Moore was a man who was unappreciated in his day. However I made it happen when I travelled to visit this great man before he passed away. If I hadn't pulled the trigger I would have missed the privilege of being in his company, if only for a brief time.

A list of those who are now unreachable in person but whom I had the privilege to spend time with: Yousuf Karsh, Arnold Newman and D.H. Moore just to name a few.

My trigger factor is what drives me. It is my burning desire, my commitment to pass on to others my brand, my purpose in leaving a footprint in the sands of time. This is the reason I write, the reason I photograph, the reason I speak. My slogan became apparent when I started teaching photography. I was told that I needed a title for my class and so the statement *Feeling more deeply about photography* was born. This is now my brand and says it all.

I wish this to be my legacy, what I will be remembered for and to move others in a similar manner.

There is so much to say. Please read my photographs with this in mind.

Most images in this book have been reproduced from the original framed photograph.

Depending on the photograph's final finish, be that on canvas, watercolour paper or other unique substrate, this will impact the texture revealed within the images illustrated in this book.

Glamour

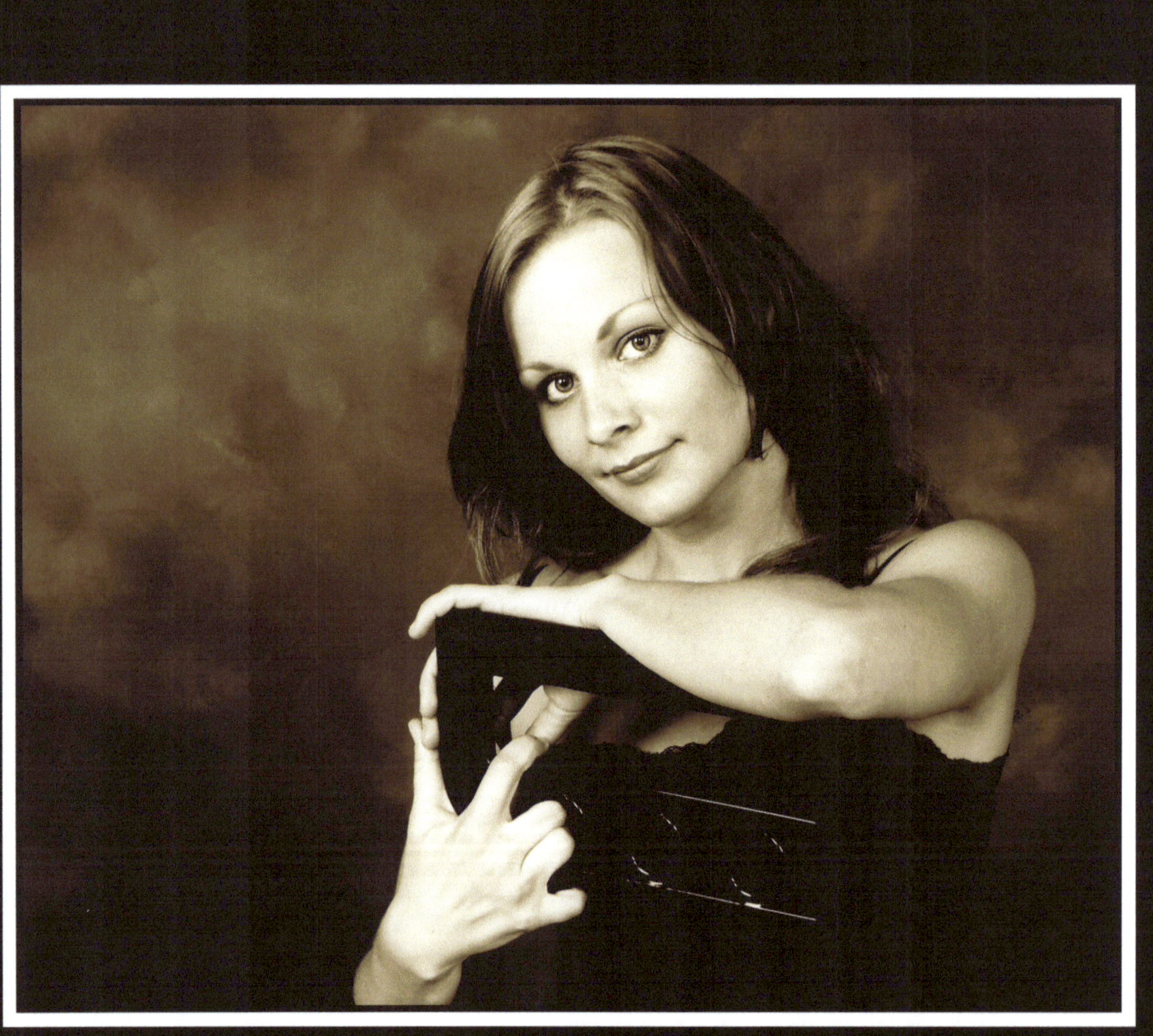

A Vision of Beauty

Mothers are so wonderful. This girl's mother came in to discuss her daughter's photograph that she had done by another photographer which had problems with head size and a few other points of concern. We had in depth consultations and she decided that I would photograph her daughter as well as her two sons for wall sized prints.

I enjoyed my time with each one, their different personalities and yet a family similar in many ways. This was evident even in the brief amount of time I spent with the mother. She is a warm and fun person whose personality could be seen in each one of her children, especially the daughter.

After choosing the photographs and ensuring the head sizes were in proportion, one image was made larger to maintain the continuity of head size as all three were to hang together on a large wall. I chose a warm black and white which appealed to the client and added a feeling outside the norm of reality. Black and white eliminates the reality of colour that we are so accustomed to seeing in our world and in our personal interpretation of reality.

The adjacent image uses my discretion and is an interpretation of the fun time experienced with this young lady who was so warm and tender and yet such an individual. Look at the body language, her hand playing with the design in the chair, her expression and the eyes and mouth in sync which implies a really genuine expression. As parents we tend to see our children in a most biased way because they are often seen as we would like them to be, not necessarily as they are with others or their friends.

Interaction sets the tone of the image and takes into consideration how we interpret it. The way we see is a result of our experiences with people and how well we know the individual. This may seem complicated but the reaction needs to be in keeping with the composition. When this young lady came in to review other images from the photo shoot she was overwhelmed because I had her image on display in the window. With a tear in her eye she exclaimed, "I am beautiful!" Why do we put ourselves down and not appreciate who we are? False impressions are given to us by the media and Hollywood as well as comments we may have heard from others and how they are interpreted. It is important to remember that we most often see ourselves in the mirror which is a reverse interpretation of what we really look like. We have heard the argument, "The photo doesn't look like me," followed by, "Oh yes it does it is a good picture!" "Oh no it isn't!" "Yes it is!" and back and forth and on it goes.

Looking at the image we can see lines, angles, shapes and design; may we learn not only from this book or this image but the reality of life. We must study by looking to see what is truly before our eyes.

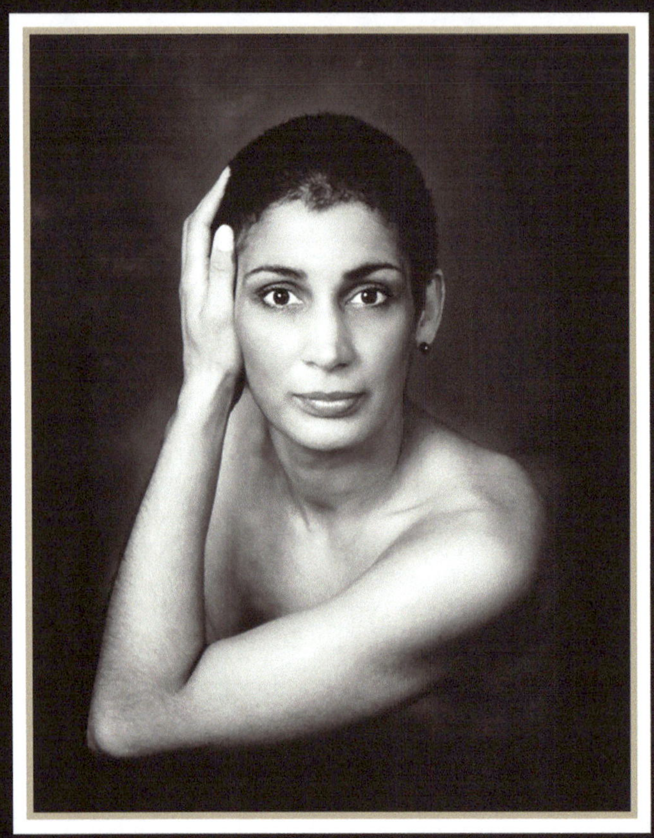

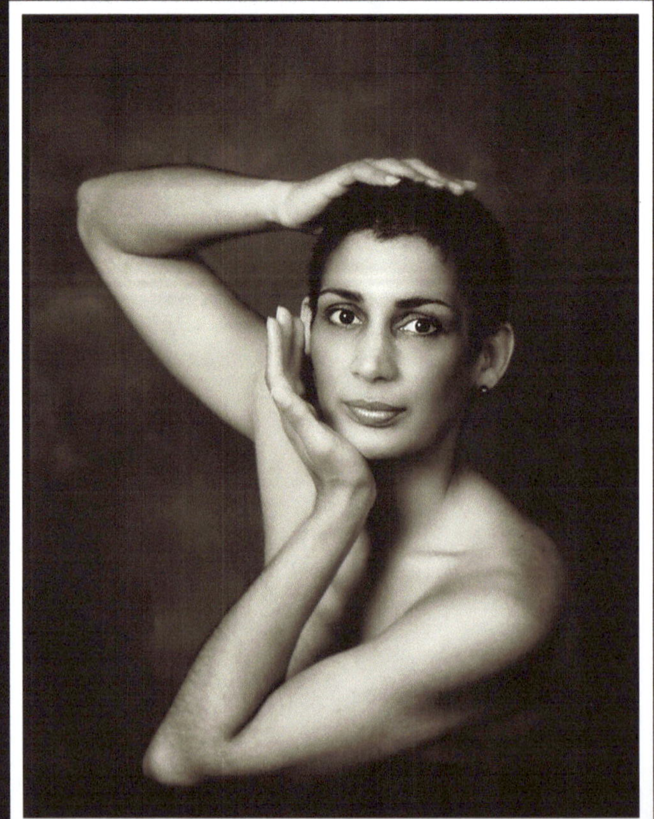

Portrait of a Selfless Act

When this young woman came into my studio I immediately noticed her very short hair. She told me that she shaved her head to raise funds for the Cops for Cancer charity. Before her hair grew in any more she wanted a photograph for her wall at home. She didn't want just a record keeping photograph but rather an image that had power. To this end she brought in some books with examples that we might explore in the photographic session.

She exudes strength, determination and power. The hand up to her face was more her idea than mine while the brown tone photo was more my idea. Exploring the image where only one hand is up, the composition is strong, framing her face, with the shoulder and arm like a triangle and her shoulder wraps around to produce a soft curve. Without a full head of hair it gives a fleshly feeling. There is nothing to hide behind, a sense of vulnerability and yet her strength lies within, in the body, in the flesh so to speak. Our true strength reveals itself in how we overcome a great deal of adversity! This image portrays real human strength with her hand flat against her head so nothing can come between. Look at her eyes, how focused they are and her lips are an echo of her eyes. For me a *true* portrait can be determined if the eyes and lips are in unison. Her eyes and lips are saying the same thing, there is no confusion here.

One ear, one hand, note everything is not visible in the black and white image, only what we wanted the viewer to see. The black background camouflages and makes it appear as though she is floating in space, darkness all around and yet the life within is so real and has great potential. There is a hidden expression, a feeling, as she looks right at you and beyond. Her head is straight up and down and her body is on an angle suggesting movement and life. What a privilege it was to photograph this wonderful woman. When working with a client I don't pose them in the traditional manner because for me there is a flow, a rhythm like music that we see with our eyes keeping the flow continuous from one image to the next.

The brown tone image is softer, more playful and fun. Look at the hands, the shape of them lightly touching with gentleness and her expression has softened as well. See the angles her arms make with her body. This image seems freer to me somehow and the brown tone makes it warmer, while the little twist of her hand by her face opens up and gives an invitation to the viewer.

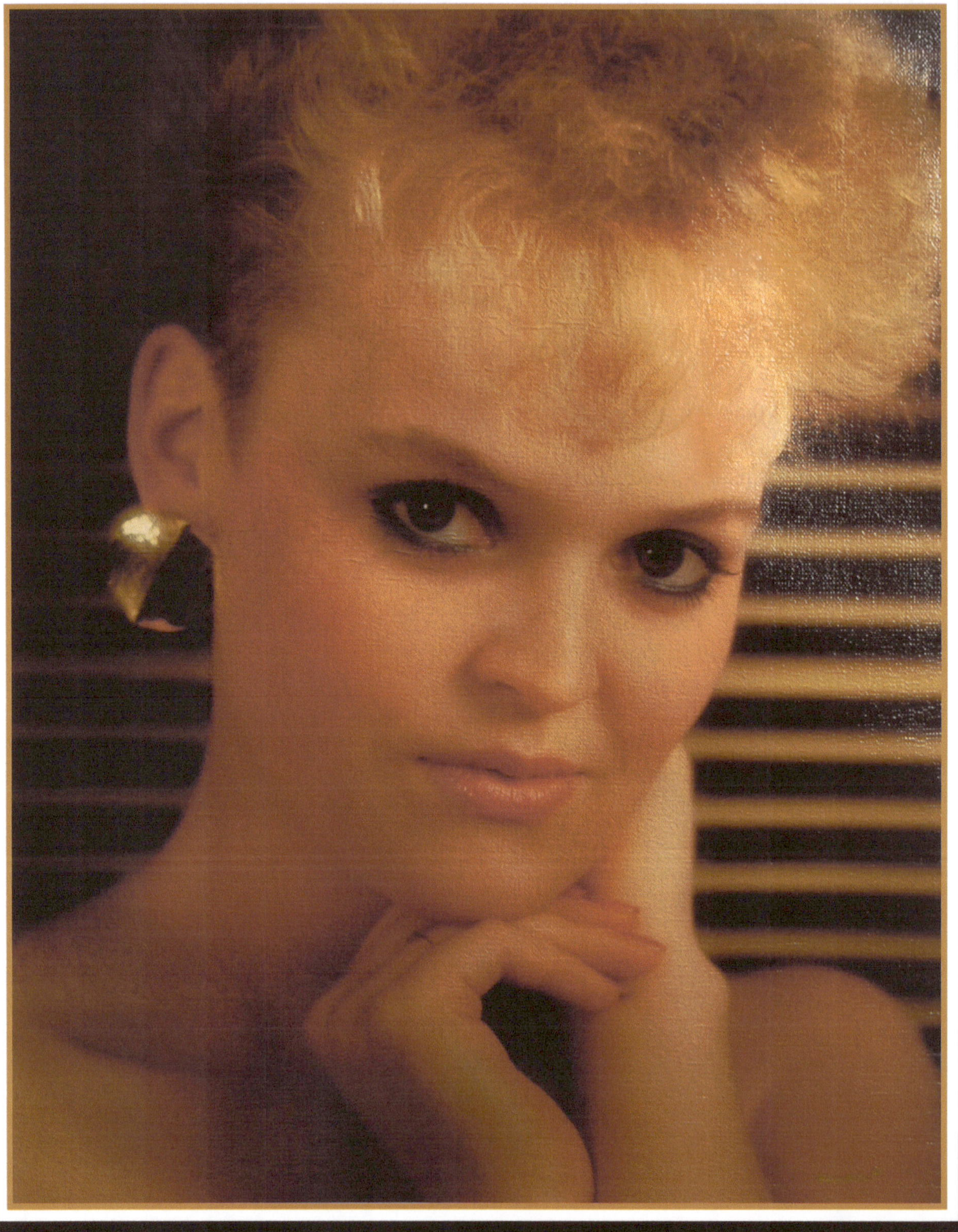

The Graduate

Over the years I have photographed many grads from all over Saskatchewan, the rest of Canada and the United States. I like oversized heads, especially when I produce grad or high school senior photographs with this unusual style. I have been criticized by other professional photographers who comment, "How can you make photos so large, bigger than life size?" My response to this question has always been, "How can you make photographs with head sizes smaller than life size?" Distortion has always been there in paintings as well as the other arts including photography. It is really a matter of proper viewing distance from the image. Study old paintings and you will be surprised how large some of the paintings were!

The largest grad photos sold in my studio were 40 by 50 inches and we sold quite a few over the years but a more popular size was 30 by 40 inches like the image on the opposite page. I am a professional photographer as well as a good salesman believing in my product and what I am able to accomplish for the client. The expression in her eyes compliments her lips and creates a pleasing image from the right viewing distance. It is important to not make the mistake of having one's client smile too forcefully as it tends to distort the face making the eyes smaller and hence very uncomplimentary.

Have you ever wondered why there were fewer smiles in paintings years ago? They refer to da Vinci's Mona Lisa as the smiling Mona Lisa. If you have been to the Louvre in Paris and viewed the painting you couldn't say that she was smiling, not ear to ear like so many grads photographed by school photographers.

My system of photographing grads was no different than my regular photography. A consultation was a must and so was a projection a day or so following the photo session to review the images. I would accomplish all three in one day for students from out of town. We had a number of loyal and energetic employees to help during these busy times but I always did all the consultations, sessions and projections myself.

The image you see was mounted on canvas as were a lot of my photographs at that time. My brother Brian operated the framing and mounting part of the business as it took skill to produce a good canvas.

What a privilege to influence young lives as well as their parents to appreciate photography in completely different ways.

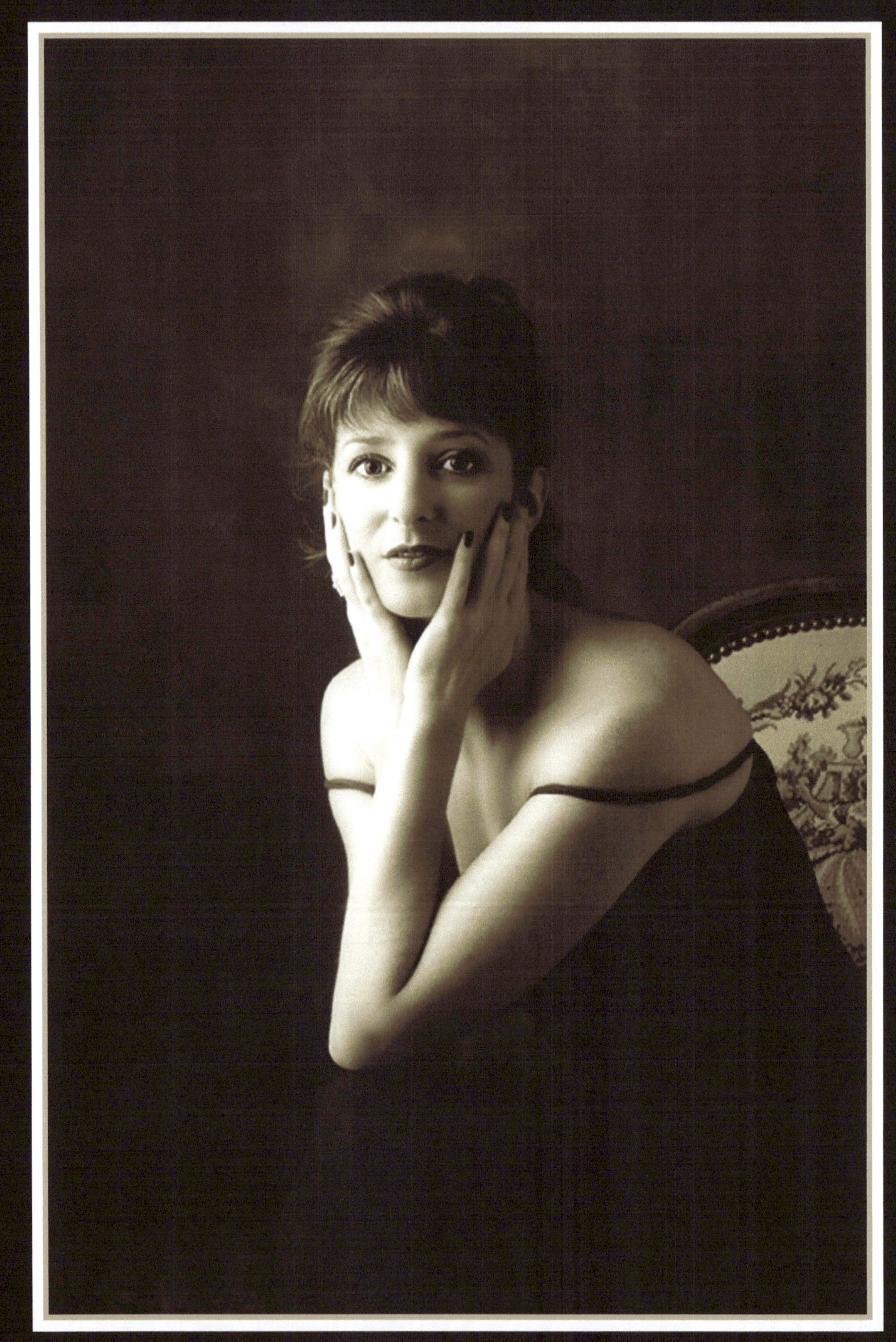

Finding her Softer Side

This woman came into my studio and wanted some modelling photos. She was only in Canada for a short time and wanted them before travelling back home to South Africa. I believe I photographed her sister's wedding.

"I like your work," she said. Words like that always give me a warm fuzzy feeling and it was a great experience to work with her. She realized that being a little older could have some drawbacks but the experience was worth it for both of us.

Being refined and slight in build made each pose easy to form and illustrate her uniqueness. I loved working with her and went the extra mile in lighting and was engrossed in our conversation. Her homeland has always fascinated me even though I have yet to travel there. South Africa, the land of beauty with wildlife beyond compare and yet a place with a tumultuous history, much poverty, the devastating effects of HIV/AIDS and so on.

Dean Collins popularized this lighting technique with translucent flats and I learned from him when I took his course in San Diego, California. Forty-one by seventy-six inches, the framework is made from PVC pipes with elastic rope. Flats can be snapped together with ease and various nylon materials can then be stretched over the frame. I loved the effect so much that I bought the whole set. I had the opportunity to judge with Dean and we once spoke at the same convention. Over the years we bumped into each other from time to time.

In photographing this woman this lighting method was used; a translucent flat on the left side facing her with power light 600 in a soft box. This added a very soft flavour to the light and complemented her complexion. A flat was also utilized as a reflector on the opposite side to fill in the shadow, wrapping the light around and still keeping the shadow side three stops or so deeper. Finally, a background light was used to add depth to the overall image.

I love to play with the positioning of hands in many of my photographs. I first observed this technique in paintings and then took a course with Don Blair who spent a great deal of time educating us about hands. The woman's hands not only help support her head but also frame her face to add the feeling of warmth and touching. The design of this photograph is like the shape of a kite, suggesting her ability to fly high in whatever her future holds.

Working with shapes allows me to continually discover more possibilities in my work. There is no end. Look at nature, in the woods, every imaginable and unimaginable shape exists to be discovered over and over again. Why are we satisfied with just a few designs repeated over and over again? Are we so confined due to others or are we too lazy to work at putting more effort into design? My poem "The Driven Man" which appeared in my first book *50 Principles of Composition in Photography* reveals that it takes more than just effort; it takes a burning desire to be driven.

May I never be too timid or lazy to go the distance whatever that is perceived to be. There is the story of a Greek runner back many hundreds or thousands of years ago who won the race and kept on running all the way home to his village to tell them of his victory. You can't just stop when you are finished, we need to go on and tell others, tell the story over and over again. To use the brand "Feeling more deeply about photography," my natural life's work is all about photography. It is ingrained, infused, imbibed; breath it in, become a Breatharian!

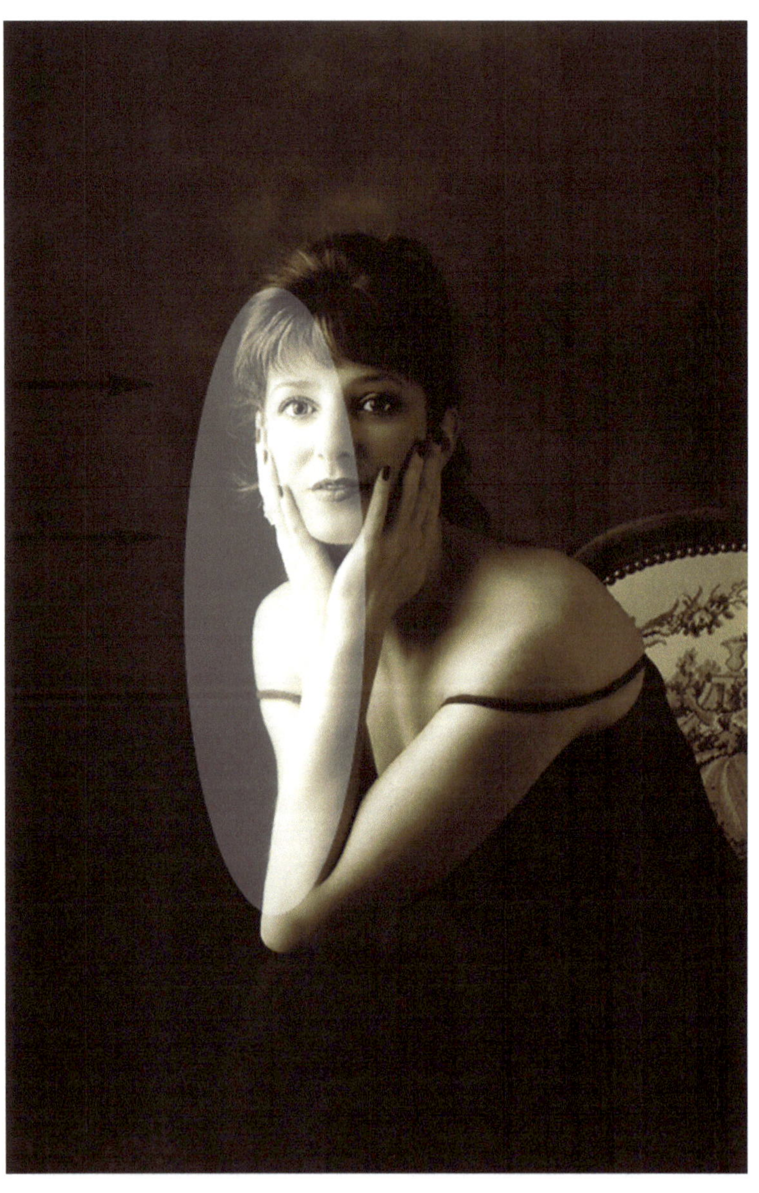

The Beauty of Children

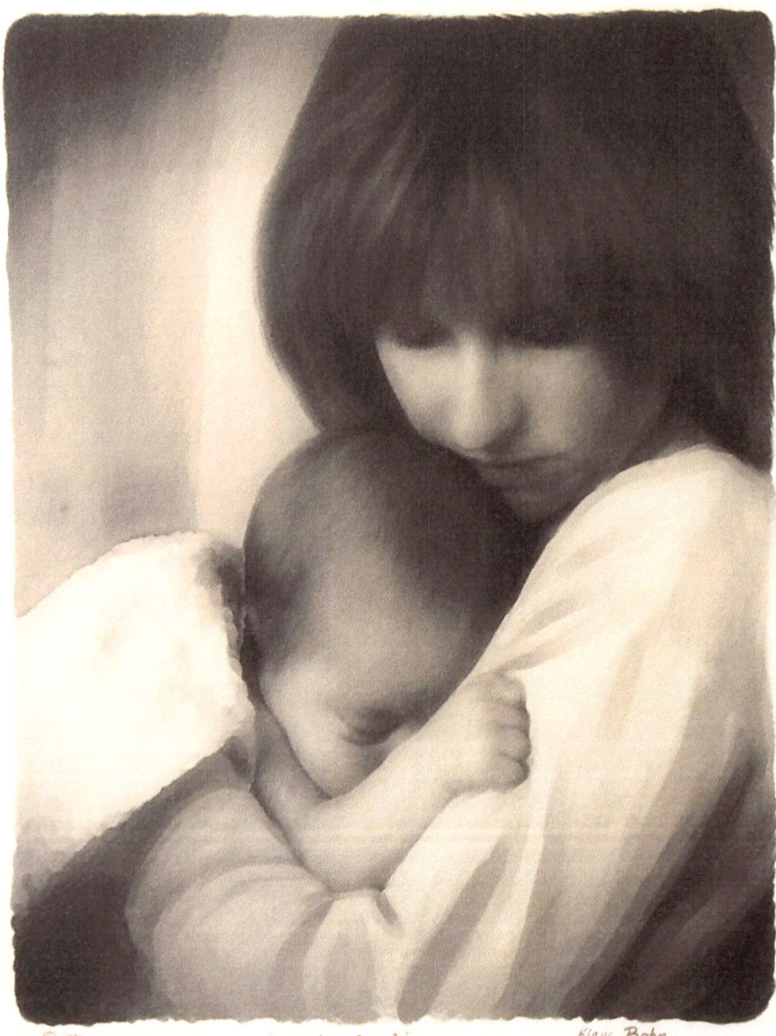
© 1996
"My Little Angel"
Klaus Bohn

My Little Angel

When this new mother came in for her consultation she was already familiar with my procedure because I had photographed her once before. I always start with a consultation first, followed by the photo session and finally a projection appointment that allows us to work together to choose the best image, size and finish. In this instance the finish was her prime interest. During our consultation she indicated that she wanted the image to have an art look. To satisfy this requirement the photo was printed on watercolour paper using Lysonic inks which are known for their longevity and have an estimated life of sixty-five to seventy-five years.

She shared a funny yet true story with me. Being a nurse in Los Angeles her friends and co-workers asked, "Why are you going to Canada? For a vacation?" "No," she said, "I'm going to see my photographer." Stunned, they asked, "Why go all the way to Canada?" She said, "Wait until you see the art piece, you will be green with envy." I don't know if it was so but I do know that both of us loved the feeling we got from looking at the finished piece.

Let's look at this photograph together and see if it means more to us than a picture, perhaps reaching beyond the barrier of a photographic print to an artistic print and even a piece of art. First we may feel the impact and yet a gentle, soft and tender impression radiates from the image. Truly every mother can feel and relate to this and we can extend this to every human being with a heart, in their own way moved with feeling.

I decided that a warm black and white would express the overall story in a way that colour could not. By eliminating the colour it forces the viewer not only to observe the natural beauty but to see beyond it and enter into the story. In this manner by eliminating what would or could interfere, each viewer is allowed to exercise their own emotion.

The down cast eyes, perhaps she is looking at her baby girl. The baby is fast asleep in the mother's gentle and protective arms, a truly safe place. What an image of ***love***. It can't be expressed in any better way; a trusting child within a complete circle of life... life begets life.

Left to right composition makes it easy for the viewer to enter into the photograph and the circular design soothes the viewer to study the image a little longer. The Mother's eyes are in the right thirds, a most powerful composition location; the golden mean to strengthen her role in child rearing. The strength of a mother can never be underestimated. In quiet solitude there is a feeling of movement by the noticeable diagonal composition in the photograph as shown in the work print with lines to help you see why I cropped and used space as I did. I love the V-shape in the image as it suggests a tight bond in the crook of the mother's arm and the circle around the baby's face and clinched fist as if she was hanging on for dear life. The gentleness of the mother's expression tells us all we need to know about her feelings as a tender loving mother. The top left space gives us breathing room to view what was captured in a split second.

It was a wonderful honour when the Art Gallery of Greater Victoria in British Columbia displayed this image along side many great masterpieces. The privilege of a photograph is that we can revisit the image over and over again, especially when displayed in a proper size to be enjoyed by all onlookers, a joy to behold.

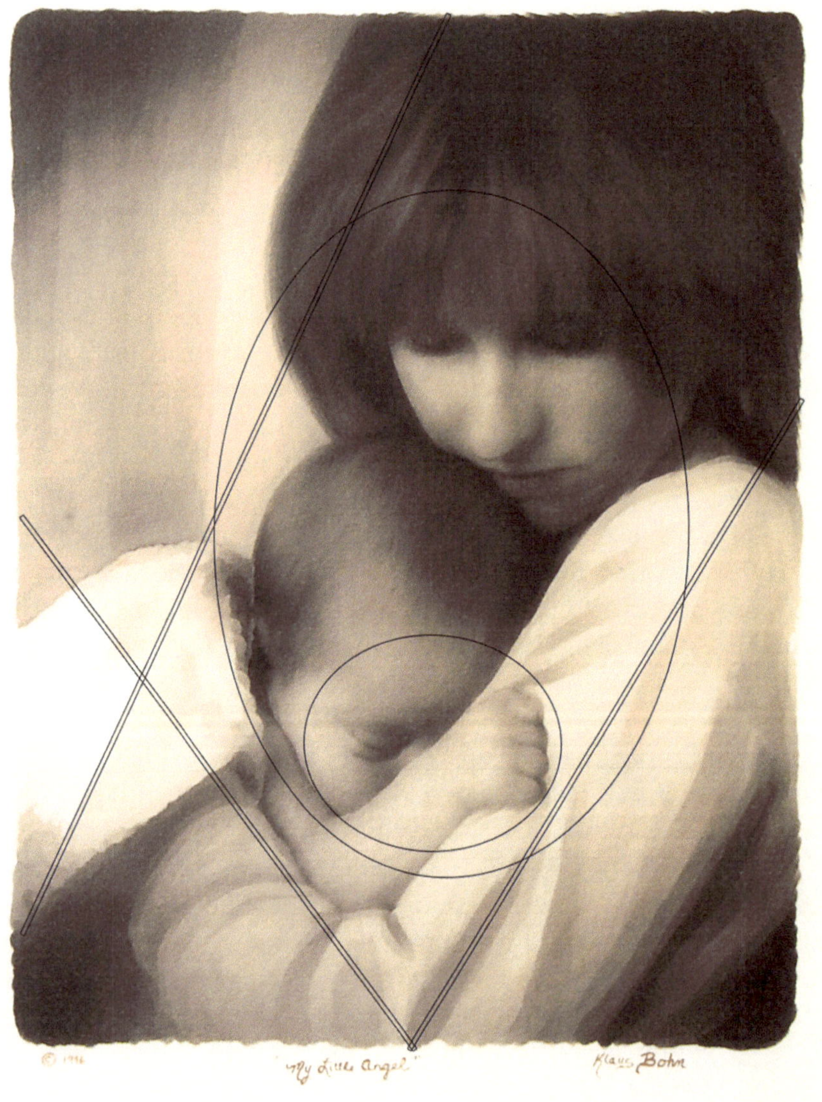

"Love is the muscle that can't be over worked;
in every relationship, in all we do and are!"
-Klaus Bohn

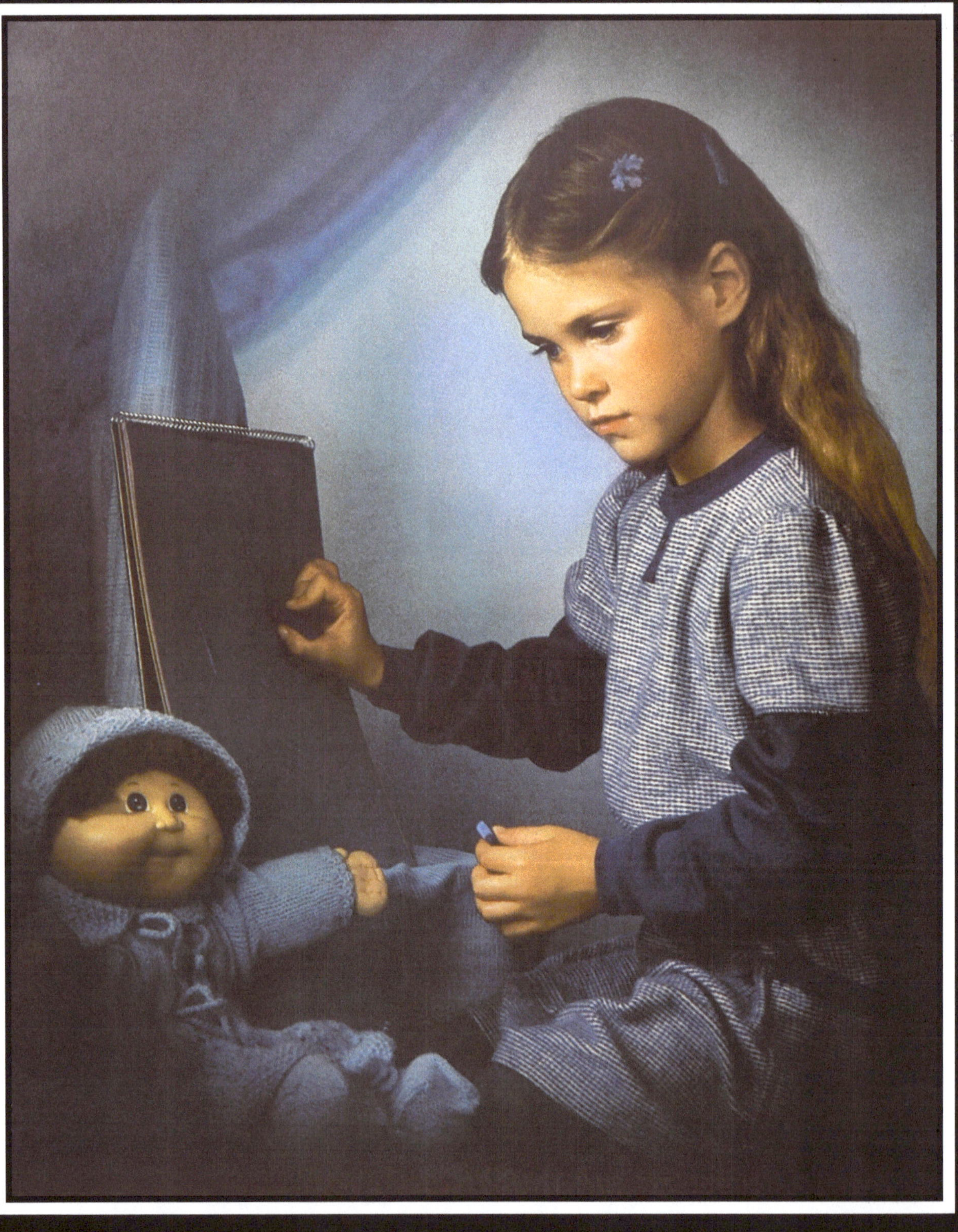

Patchy Blues

When I saw my daughter, Tammy, drawing her Cabbage Patch Kids doll it inspired me to set up a staged photograph that I eventually turned into a very popular poster which is still selling to this day. One of these posters is even in Magic Crystal Valley, the largest Cabbage Patch Kids Museum in the world with over 6,000 dolls on display.

This was a tense moment for Tammy because she was proud that I wanted her to model for me again and to make it believable, she concentrated on what I told her to do. "Look at the doll and envision how you will draw her; this will be a famous picture of you, your doll and the art work you have just begun," I told her.

I love the feeling and purpose, its intensity. As some of us will remember, there was a time when Cabbage Patch Kids dolls caused a mania all over the free world, well the western world perhaps. People lined up for hours just to purchase a doll for their child or for a collection or just to say, "I have one!"

The set up took time but capturing this image went quickly because it would have been impossible to hold this moment for very long, especially with someone so young. I needed to be ready and coach her with the right verbal cues and tonality. Timing is everything in photography. Having studied Neuro-Linguistic Programming or NLP I discovered how our body language, voice, eye movement and just about everything that is by definition non-word communication does in fact communicate. The meaning of words is not always accurate to the listener and it is only when we interpret the words using both sound and body language that they suggest true communication.

Look at the Animal Kingdom. Until recently it was believed that animals, birds and fish couldn't send messages to one another but we are learning that communication is not only by words. True communication is sent by our emotions, suggested through our body language and just the sounds we make have an influence, communicating without saying a word. My friend William McKay told me about Baba Hari Dass, a silent monk who has not spoken since 1952 and communicates by writing on a small chalkboard. He has taken his vow of silence to a higher level and communicates not only through the written word but also by his powerful presence. I'm sure every word is thought out before it is written. Wouldn't this world be different if we all communicated in this manner?

Another friend of mine, Jasmine Kinnear, is a Feline Behaviour Consultant and has written several books about cats (www.confessionsofacatbreeder.com). When I read some of Jasmine's books I was totally unaware how much cats communicate. Shortly thereafter I was given, or should I say persuaded, to look after my daughter's cat when she moved to Victoria, British Columbia. This was to be a temporary arrangement until she settled into her new place with her cousin Heidi. The cat's meow changes in the morning. Her meow is different as if to say, "Good morning, now feed me." When she wants attention her tone changes once again. I need to learn her language as we all need to learn the language of our family, friends and spouses. If we could only learn to communicate with one another all over the world like Baba Hari Dass we would have peace of mind and peace on earth.

Getting back to the Cabbage Patch Kids doll image, let's explore what it is trying to communicate. Tammy is looking at the doll as if it was alive. Her doll's hands out stretched as if she is welcoming the world into her life through this image. Tammy holding the chalk in her left hand suggests the colour of the doll's clothing and in her right hand a darker coloured chalk outlines the doll's profile. The tonal value is indicated throughout the image, with Tammy's clothing in a different hue but still in the blue family.

"Peace of mind, peace on earth"
-Baba Hari Dass

"Every time someone tells me
how sharp my photographs are,
I assume they aren't very interesting.
If they were they'd have more to say."
-Author Unknown

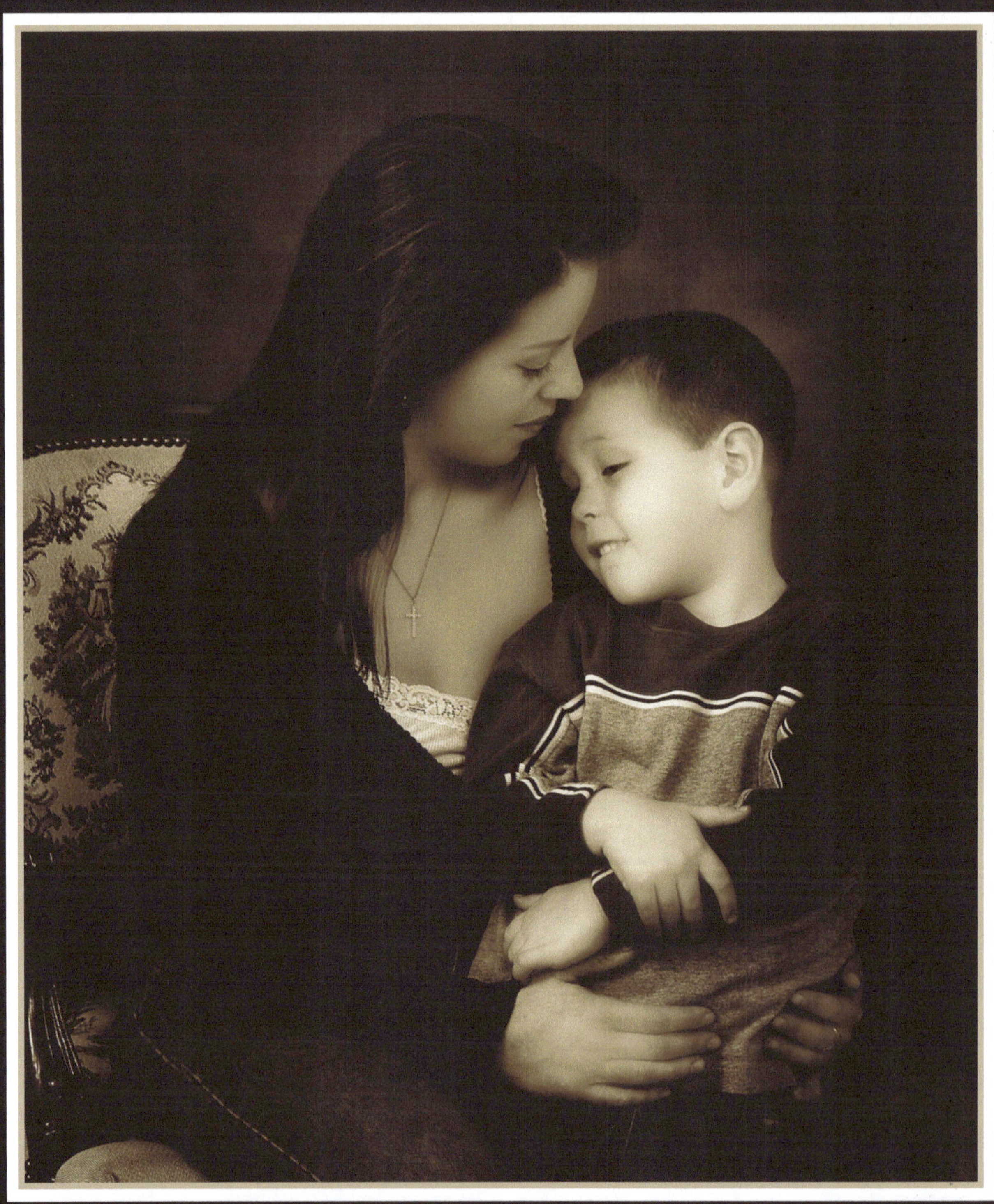

A Tender Embrace

To see a child so full of life is a comforting treat. We see motivation in young lives and hope that this drive will remain even into their senior years. To accomplish this we need to keep up the pace and strive to increase our awareness to continue and press on. While walking quickly in a mall one day an older gentleman, or at least older than me, reached out and said, "Sonny I wish I could walk as fast as you!" To keep our youthfulness has to do with what we put into our bodies and how we move through the day, so-called exercise. I do not like the words diet or exercise. It should not be a diet in the traditional sense but rather a change in our eating habits, and a way of life that fills us with energy. We also need to include movement to be youthful and able, walking, moving and stretching like a child.

This mother had her hands full with a lively child who had energy to spare. To work with a high energy person we need to work fast, letting the scene develop but anticipating and always ready to act. I had to know the child's next move. As has been said of Wayne Gretzky, he skates where the puck will be, not where it is; this made him one of the greatest hockey players in history, Mr. 99.

To see the relationship between mother and son is a warm experience, a privilege. Hopefully we can all enjoy such a relationship, tender and true at any age, especially if we are able to mend fences along the way. By looking into the child's face we can see so much more than words can tell. We need to look and see and enjoy. It is a learning curve of sorts but in doing so, may we all become students of body language including the face and tonality of our voice. Let it be so.

Let's look at the image and see how tenderness and mischief are etched on the child's face; with Mom holding the one she loves no matter the challenges he might bring into her life. Their bodies turned towards each other create a sensation of love. The mother's eyes travel as a diagonal line to her son and the boy pulling in close as if he was comfortable enough to go to sleep and yet his eyes move us down further to complete the design of thirds, their heads being in a very strong position. Look at the circle their arms and heads form. The young boy folded his hands automatically without any coaching as I worked with them both and they responded to create a wonderful image. As professionals we *must* learn to not only influence the subject but also react to the subject. From left to right, the chair helps to bring in the viewer's eye on a roller coaster ride from the chair up to Mom's head and then down to her son's head. Following the arms and hands makes the image complete and keeps us looking at the photograph just a little longer to satisfy our feeling and appreciation of what went into creating this image for their wall.

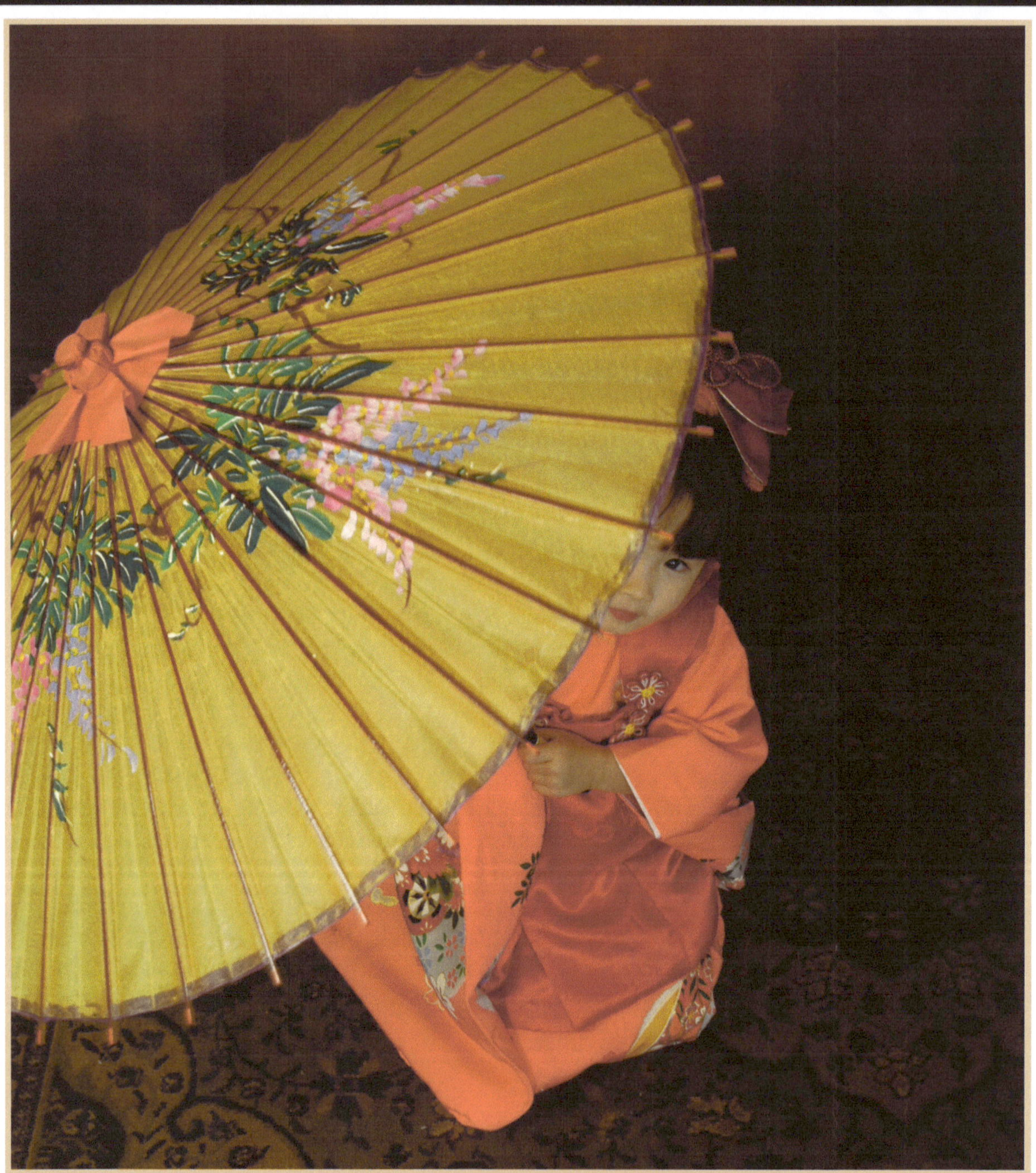

Peek-A-Boo

There are songs about little girls which reach out and touch our hearts in so many ways because as parents we feel the song's words. Children need to be hugged and touched and kissed so that the bond is forever strengthened even through times of heartbreak. They should never feel disappointed, selfish or unacceptable because after all we are only flesh and blood. Your pain is my pain, your joy is my joy; may a parent love their child without regret or sorrow.

I have always enjoyed children, especially my own, and through the Professional Photographers of Canada (PPOC) I earned my Accreditation in Child Photography. Children are such a blessing as they perpetuate human existence with a little bit of ourselves ingrained in our children thereby rendering us immortal. Growing up my daughter told me, and I might say it was obvious when she became a teenager, that being like her Dad was not cool. Today, as a grown woman she says, "I know I'm like you and I have accepted it." As her Dad I'm glad and thank her.

When this little girl came in with her parents for a photo session she was so cute, so beautiful, prim and proper. Of course more traditional pictures for the grandparents were taken first and then we tried to capture a concept we discussed during the consultation: a beautiful portrait for their wall at home. The parents did not choose this image as their wall portrait; however this image is illustrated here because I felt and liked her shyness, her hidden beauty coming out like a flower and one day she will fully blossom as a young lady. During the stages of life, from birth to the end of our days, we can always see beauty but it needs to be in the eyes of the beholder. We need to learn to appreciate every little nuance as beauty can be seen in how a child ties their shoes or just tries something for the first time.

When studying this photograph the composition is strong. Like most of my images the shape of this photograph does not fit the standard four by six inch concept. Her placement is such that by cutting some of the umbrella off, it balances the fact that only part of her face is showing. Cropping the image enables us to appreciate the subtle strength of her placement. You may see and feel her shyness and yet she shows an interest in what is going on from underneath the umbrella. Conversely, the image was not cropped on the right side because it was necessary to create a feeling of balance and space.

As indicated in the work print image on the following page, the larger circle shields her, as it were, and the smaller circle reveals over half her face. This indicates that the little girl's interest is focused on what is beyond her safe hiding place; her playful yet curious manner is so overwhelming. May we all thrive from this shy curiosity, a small measure of safety and a larger measure of a child-like curiosity.

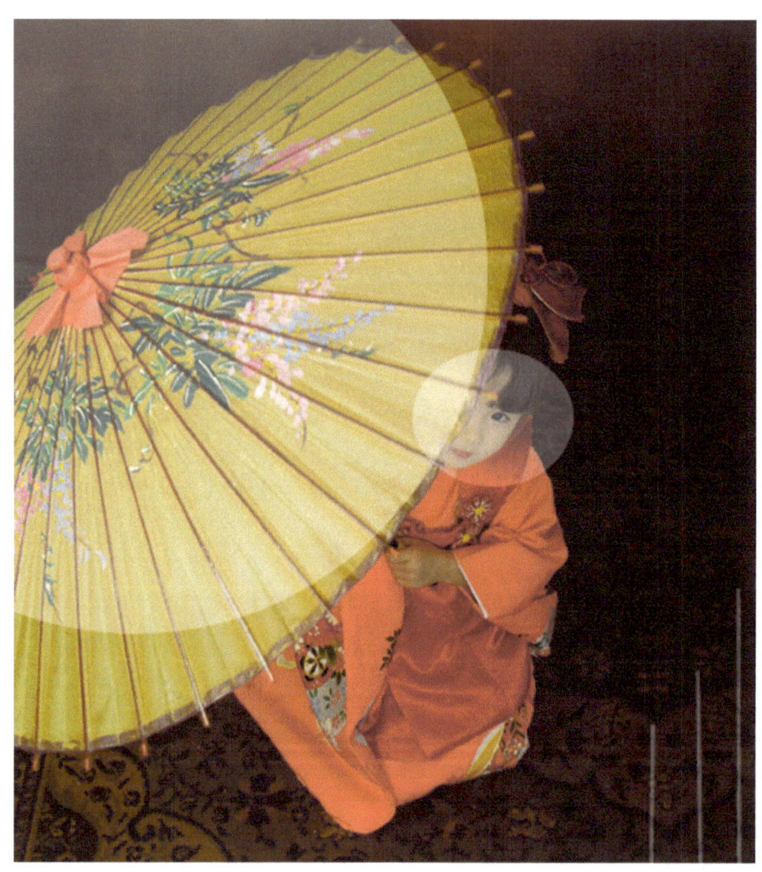

"May we never grow up and lose our creative purpose in life."

-Klaus Bohn

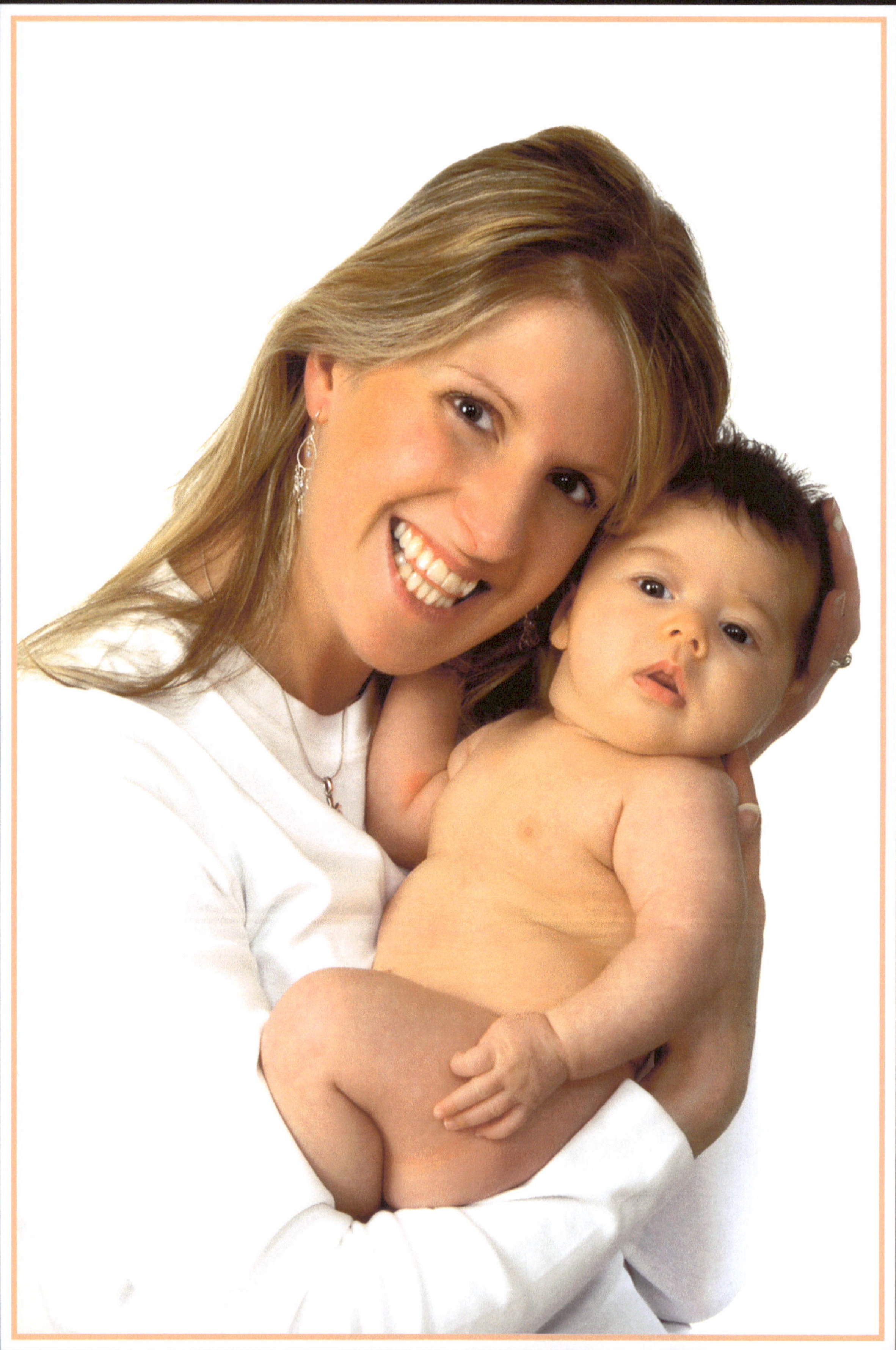

A Treasured Moment

When this mother and daughter arrived the baby was fast asleep. How wonderful because we were able to capture the beautiful baby as we wanted – the look of innocence and beauty of a sleeping infant. I love to photograph very young babies with mom or dad separately. Perhaps like most mothers her motherly instinct was evident as we began to work together; it was a cordial influencing of each other with kind and positive words. Capturing emotions and body parts, the baby's little hands and feet were so small, perfect, cute and lovely. In time the baby awoke and now we started to photograph eyes and expressions of emotion. She was a very happy little girl full of joy and life.

During the consultation I mentioned that smaller smiles or no smile at all can show real feeling in subtle ways that is sometimes otherwise inexpressible. When we reviewed the images the mother agreed but we kept coming back to this one which is not my usual way of photographing people. I felt that this was a good example to illustrate how we can break our own rules and come up with an image that satisfies both the creator and perhaps even the subject. Maybe the viewer will also be satisfied as they study this image.

When we look at how happy the mother is to have a perfect baby and the trust the infant shows as the mother holds her close to her face, there is no fear in the baby's face, just a feeling of comfort and satisfaction. The little girl has no concerns about being nude or if her Mom will take care of her. This relationship is expressed in perfect harmony, it is beauty personified!

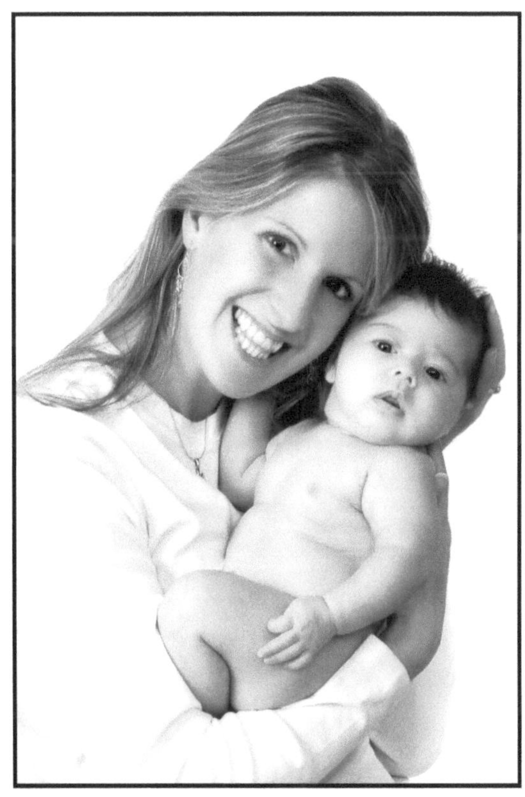

The large smile shows the happiness and thankfulness of a loving mother and the baby's expression is priceless, captured for all time, to be relived over and over again. What a wonderful treasure.

The same image is reproduced here in black and white because I wanted to reveal the difference in perception. Viewing colour relates to reality whereas black and white has a dimension all its own; thinking outside the box and creates a feeling of composition and lines. I like both but for different reasons. By using the same image it helps to see the difference and appreciate perhaps why we would choose one over the other.

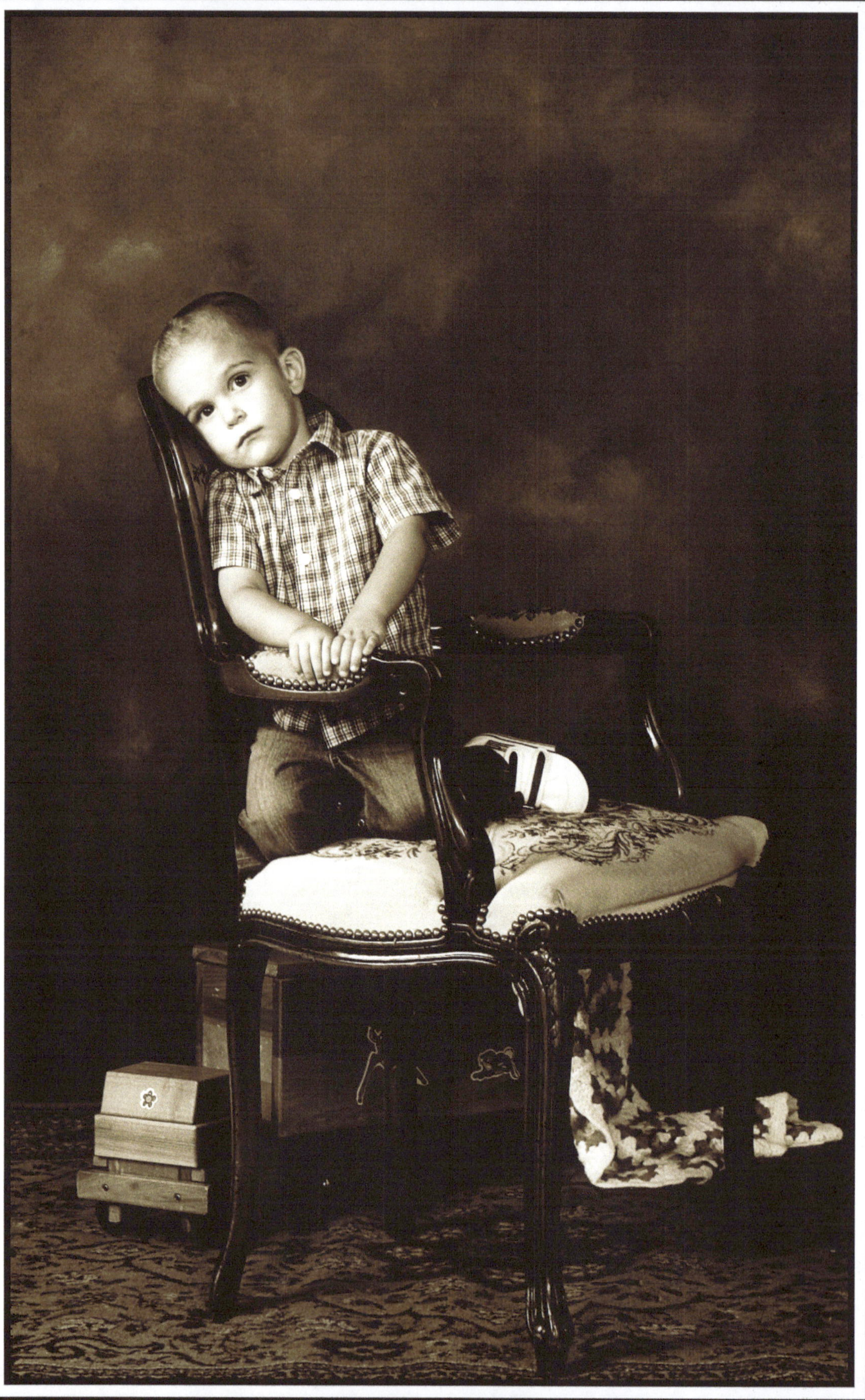

A Beloved Grandson

A few years earlier this boy's grandmother brought in her granddaughter to be photographed and together we made an artistic image to hang with her paintings. This time she brought in her grandson with the desire that I capture his look of resistance and independence. Boys will be boys, as the saying goes.

We photographed him playing with his toys, happily smiling and having a good time. Then I wanted the mood to change and accomplished this quickly by separating him from his toys, including the big truck his grandfather gave him. The mood became intense and had the impact I was hoping for as the little boy's facial expression changed to match what his grandmother had described. It was not quite a pout but perhaps a sense of defiance came through and revealed itself in his eyes.

The overall flavour was interesting; he was photographed in colour and then I felt the urge to turn the image black and white. However when I changed it into a brown tone, the image spoke to me and in that moment realized I had captured the feeling the client wanted. By adding contrast it gives us a stronger feeling towards the image.

Looking at the work print you can see the difference in the brown tone and the change of mood. The image's strength is revealed by the young boy's closeness to the left edge. He is positioned in the top thirds with his hands gripping the chair's arm and leaning hard against the back of the chair. The movement is to the left with an almost exaggerated space on the right to give the viewer a sense of mood and emotion. What is read into this image depends on the viewer; how well we know photographic composition, the stepping stones of communication in our profession, will determine what is understood.

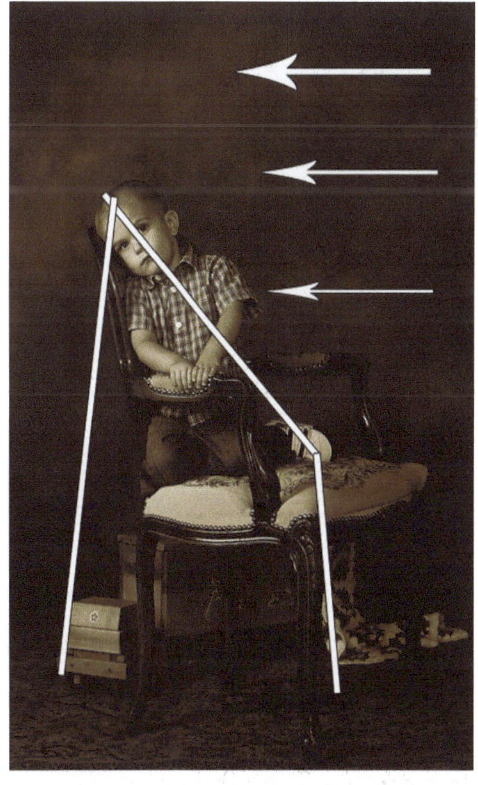

The arrows make the image seem more intense and out of the norm. Life is made up of unusual experiences that don't always follow the usual, the ordinary or the simplest path. May we learn to enter into the complex elements of life, what is unknown and unseen by us.

Let us be opened minded, willing to take into our minds that which can expand our vision and our understanding of life. Our lives are a continual experience of learning, seeing and feeling.

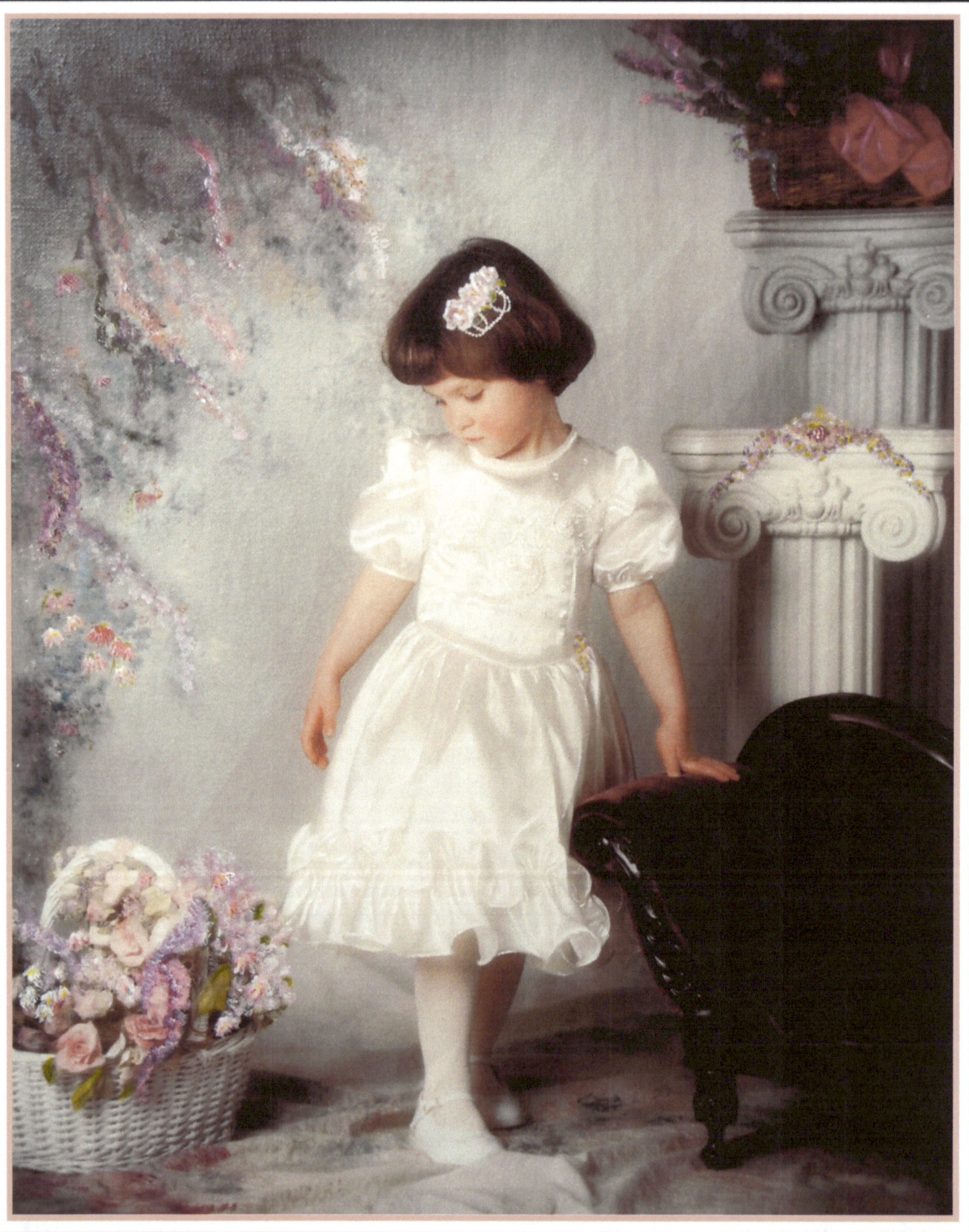

What Little Girls Are Made Of

This little girl and her mother came in for a consultation. I always recommend that parents bring the child with them for the consultation, especially if the child is to be photographed alone, so there can be a separation from mother even if it is just a short distance.

As I spoke with the mother the little girl amused herself with some toys I had on hand just for these purposes. It also sets a pattern so that when she came back it wasn't a frightening experience. Remembering how she played with the toys, it will be a fun experience again and the child will be in a positive frame of mind.

I helped the mother choose this image as a twenty-four by thirty-inch photo laminated on canvas. Using oil based paints we painted directly on the finished canvas; just enough to enhance the image. The mother wanted a painterly feel to the art piece; something that would not only stand out but also be a conversation piece, art for her wall which she could afford. The mother understood how much original works of art cost, especially from someone with a reputation. I'm not talking about me here but a renowned painter. It was a great opportunity to put together a photographic art piece.

Let us look at the design first. The little girl is not looking into the camera but instead is taken with her surroundings, as it should be. She is all dressed up and the flowers on the left drew her attention. Looking at her face the composition is a two thirds because her eyelid on the right side is kept in the mask of her face and the nose does not break her cheek line. This is important when photographing a classic image like this one. The barrette in her hair, the flowers in the baskets, the background and the pillars were painted to enhance them and give it a more three dimensional feeling. Some light oil paints were also added to her dress, especially the little sequins. The background was chosen because it suited the clothes she wore. The props, the flowers and the pillars work well for composition and the side of the little sofa help to complete the design.

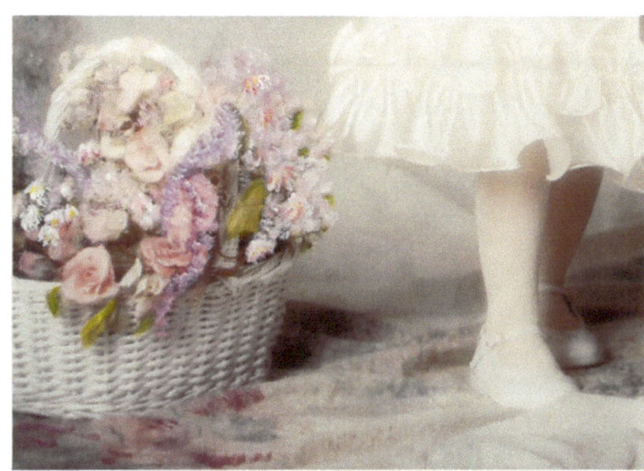

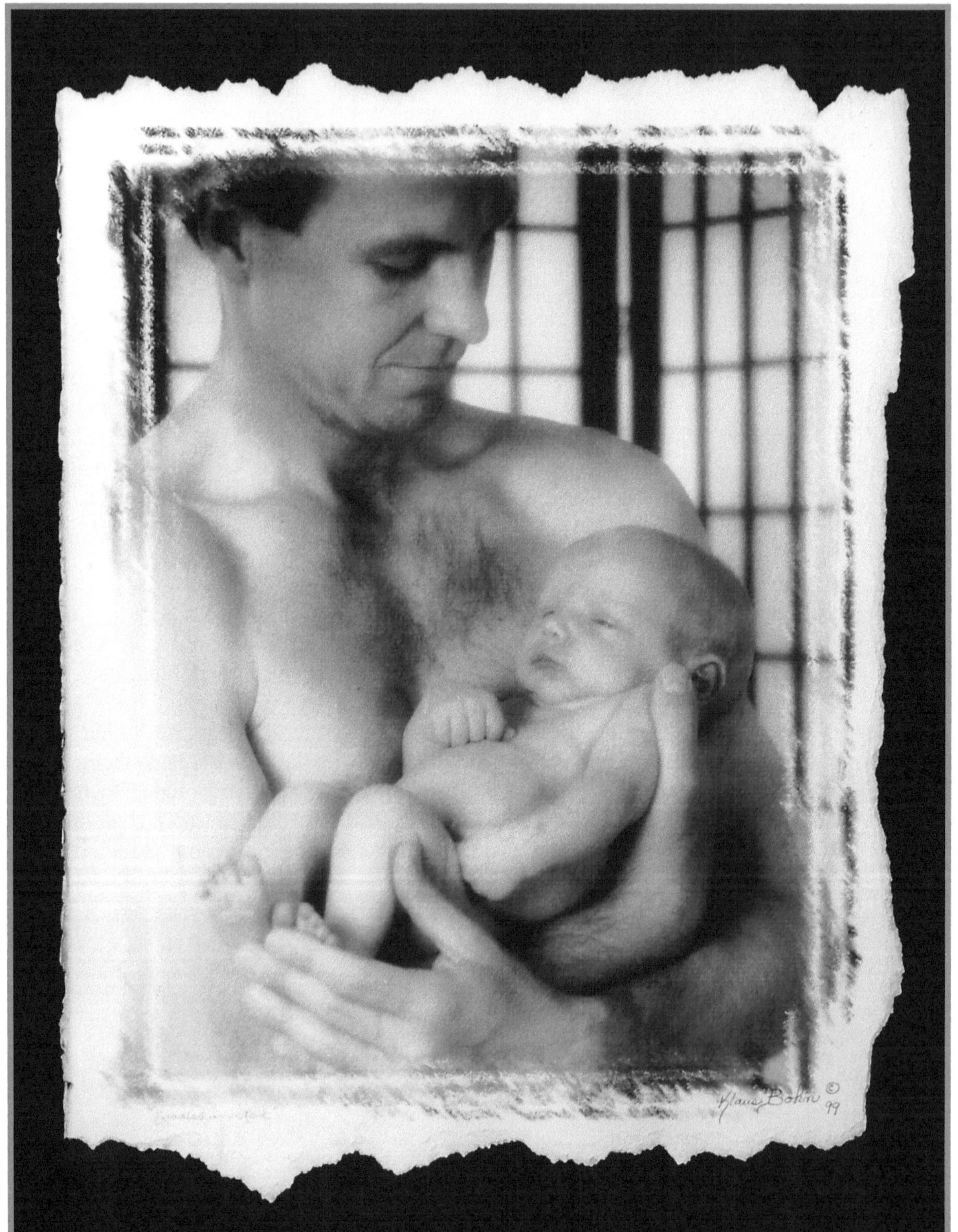
Klaus Bohn © 99

Cradled in Love

How sweet it is to see a father cradling an infant so lovingly in his arms, what a sight to behold. His wife held their first born daughter in a watercolour photograph I had done two years earlier. When their son was born the father was thrilled at the opportunity to have the same privilege of hanging this photograph along side the other image.

Please note that the woman featured in the image entitled *My Little Angel* is not this man's wife.

When we study the image we can see into the father's heart. See how close he is holding the baby's head to his heart? The father is looking at *his son* in admiration and with manly love. The baby is half asleep, so comfortable in his Daddy's arms and his little fists are representing strength in becoming a man some day. The eye line of the father leads us right to the child so there is no mistaking that this child is his and the pride he exudes. Notice the finger tips of the father's hand gently touching his son's tiny feet and those beautiful little toes, all ten of them. Holding the baby securely, in a soft masculine way we can see the father. To soften the overall image I chose the composition on the left side. This is a less dominant position, with the father's head in the thirds of the golden mean and just a little above, showing that there is a kindness from within. In this manner this image would compliment his wife's photograph which was composed on the other side, similar to the example of *My Little Angel.*

The background is strong and fitting as the image displays the complete photograph in a graphic way. Cropping into the father's head strengthens the overall image, representing masculinity which this man really had in abundance. I can't over emphasize this strongly enough because he worked on the oil pipelines. Using a rough edge around the total image we can see or feel the power and ruggedness and it adds to the power of the watercolour photograph.

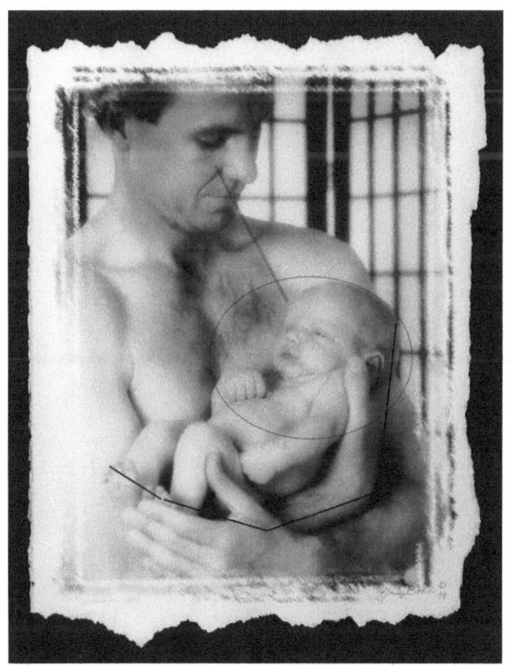

The *love* of a father so deeply seen in this one photograph, no more was needed; in full expression, nothing hidden, no shyness.

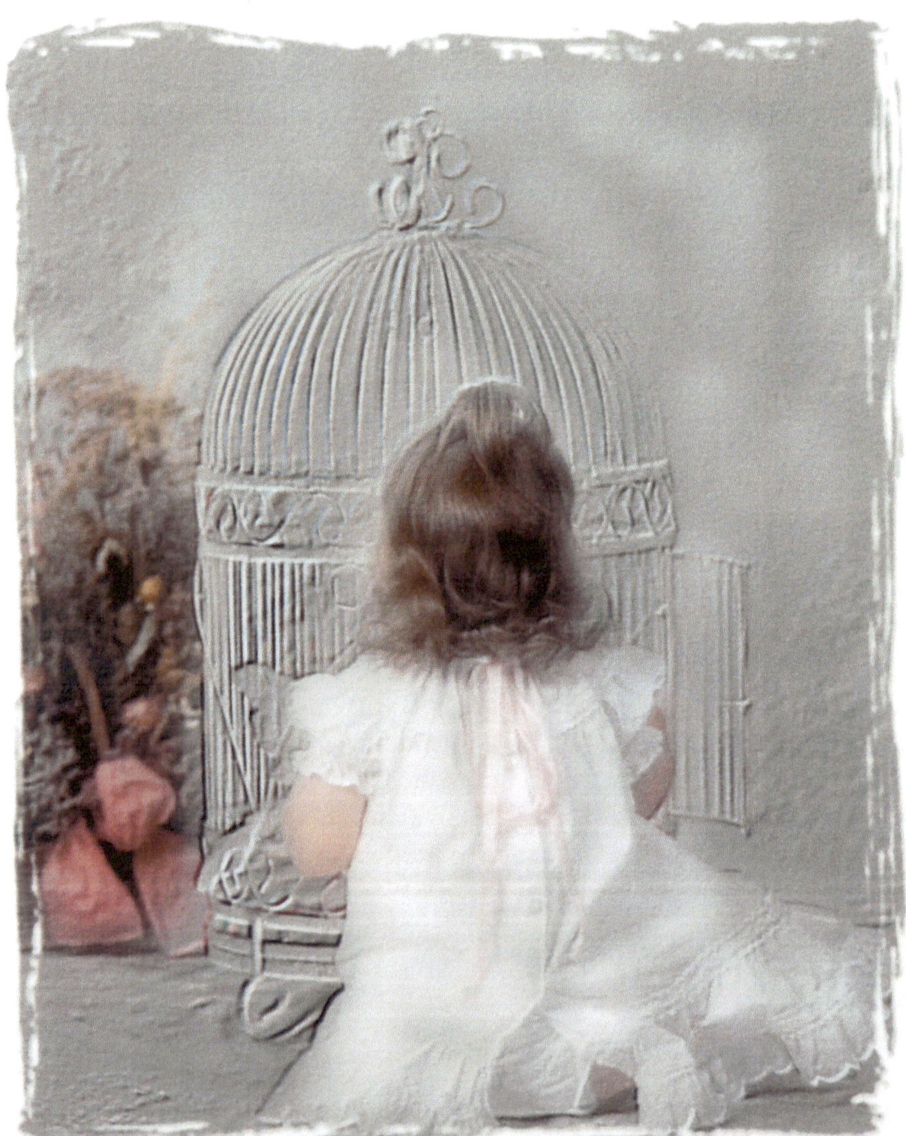

The Bird Cage

Children are fascinated by toys of all sorts, real or unreal like this bird cage with fake birds inside. It may be difficult for a young child to know if the birds are real or not. The fascination still exists, to open the door and see if the birds can be caught or will they fly out? I'm not sure what was in this little girl's mind at the time but nevertheless she was intrigued with this prop. She may never have seen nor had the chance to get this close to something so different.

Photography is not just about the face. A lady come into my studio and said, "I don't hang photographs on my walls. I only hang art on my walls." Then she saw this image and said, "Now that I would hang!" She subsequently flew in her granddaughter from Portland, Oregon, and I photographed a similar style portrait not showing the little girl's face. The image was printed on watercolour paper but she wanted it much larger than the original. To her this was art because she had not seen photography like this before as most photographers in portrait studios show faces.

As I have said so often in my classes, "A portrait is something that portrays a feeling or emotion, positive or negative. The art piece doesn't care if you like it or not because it just is."

Why do we need to see the face? Why do we want to recognize the person who we probably wouldn't know anyway, as is often the case with many old images? The Mona Lisa is an image that comes to mind. Her value has no impact upon whether we know her or not, the value is given to her because of written history which has glamorized this painting over and above all others.

Look at this portrait again and *look*, really look! The art in this portrait is revealing an emotion even if we don't see the expression on her face but we can imagine it can't we? Look at the design, the composition, that which holds our attention for longer than we would suppose and then look at the image again. Feel the excitement that we can imagine is within this little girl. Her back communicates to us because of her dress, her diaper, her hair and what is beyond the cage including the flowers and somehow we hardly see the painted background.

Study the work print and see the cut out of the flowers and cage. The door is open and she is positioned to the right just in front of the door reaching in. We embossed the cage and flowers adding texture and depth to the overall image. The lines are only there to break down that part of the image, pulling it apart as it were, to see the layering effect fitting together as a whole. The edging is softened with lines sketched into the image. We tore the edges of the paper giving a feeling for the paper as if it came from a roll, torn out and used as artists in the olden days used scraps of wood, cloth, canvas, paper or even a wall as was the case for Leonardo Da Vinci's *The Last Supper*.

As we observe this photograph, all this happens quickly and we can only see this utilizing our intuition which can be enhanced through practice. The correct term is, "We are practicing photographers."

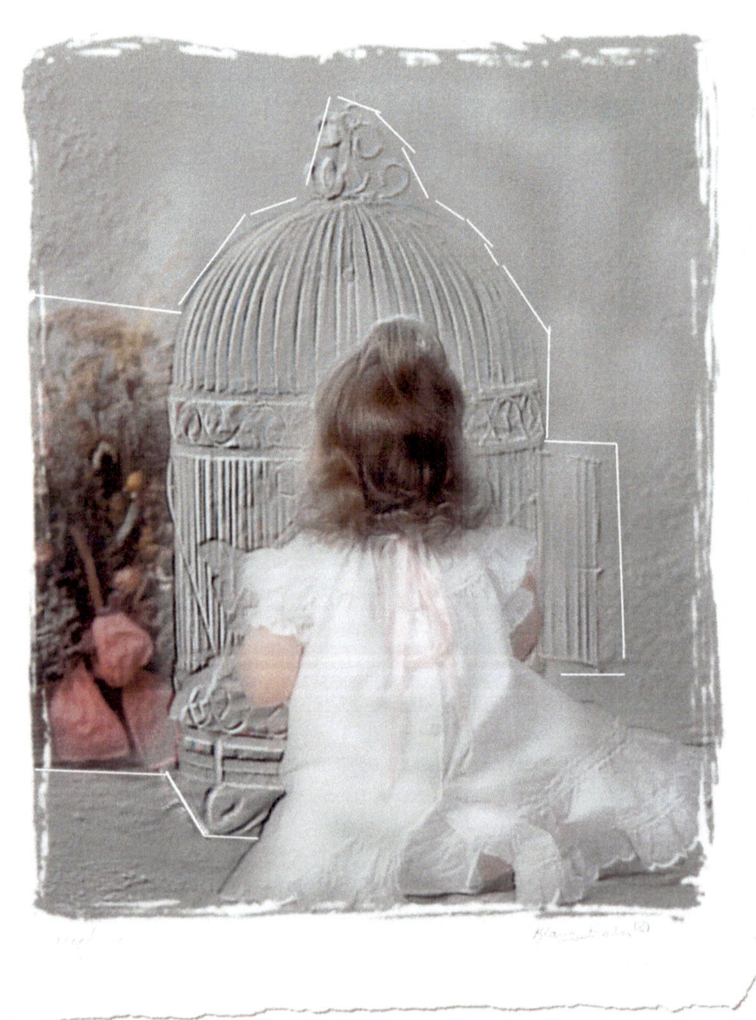

Loving Couples

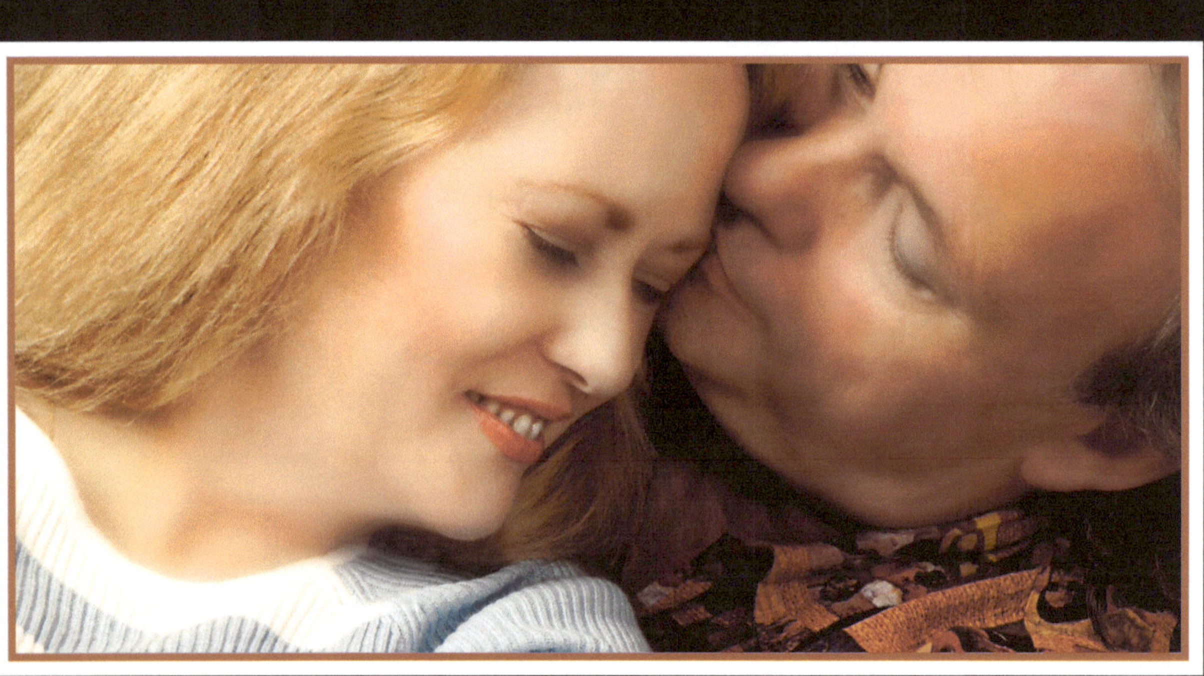

High School Reunion

"I want you more than I need you, but both are true!"
-Klaus Bohn

This couple just walked in and wanted their photograph taken. I noticed their relationship was very playful but I couldn't put my finger on it until they gave me a glimpse of their story.

"We were together in the same classes in high school," they both blurted out. "At our 30th high school reunion we bumped into each other and now we are a couple!"

They wanted a photograph revealing this intense joy which was bubbling over and could not be contained. Their body language, faces and even the quiver in their voices spoke volumes about what was taking place in this renewed relationship.

Of course I had to ask how sincere they were to have a proper photograph made. It has been my experience that money always separates the serious clients from those who are not so determined or educated about photography. He knew by the work on display in my studio that there would be a cost. He said, "I have a business and I know it costs. We like your work because it is spontaneous, so how much?" I told them and it was agreed that we would go ahead and do this *right now*. They looked in the mirror and got ready. I really wasn't but as they say, "Never let them see you sweat," and away we went.

They showed me their passion. It was an unbridled and physical passion. Need I say more? As they complied to the poses, I gave them lots of space to express themselves, twisting and turning – grabbing shots as they showed their excitement. How refreshing and movie-like, a love story right before my eyes. My responsibility was to capture emotion, body language and facial expressions; all this in a nutshell or in one image. How? To be a professional means that one can work under pressure and not faint or lose one's creativity. I knew what I hoped to get from this photo session. Also with some work on the computer it would allow me to crop, enhance and even exaggerate their form, the tilt and the passion that I felt from them.

When you study this image keep in mind what I said above. They gladly purchased a very large wall sized canvas. In fact it may have been too large or oversized as some would say. He said, "I knew that you could do it, express our hearts." In a photograph we are not only working against time but also personalities and untrained individuals; this without prep work compounds our job, our profession and our art. Satisfaction is gleaned from sources we least expect: our peers, perhaps artists and the ordinary person who just loves what we have done. Even more so, can it or will it stand the test of time and live on in the future? We will never know because life is too short; only history will bear out this accomplishment if it is to be so.

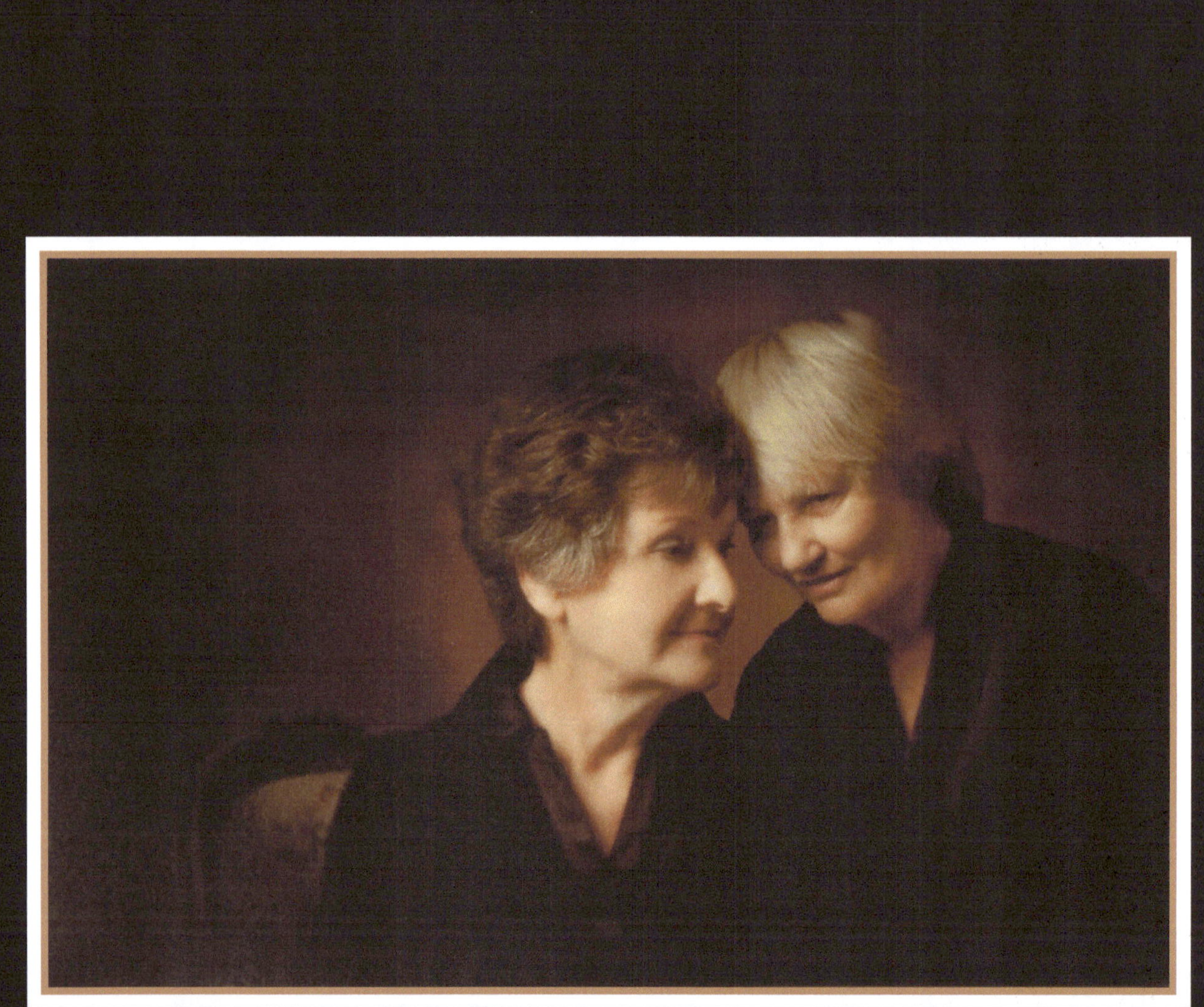

A Reflection of Thought

Two Dutch ladies came into my studio requesting information about my services but more importantly how we mount our photographs on canvas. Their interest lay in art because of the great art history of the Netherlands. They had a great eye and were able to appreciate my ability, my talent.

When I described what I had in mind they were eagerly receptive and enthusiastic to book the appointment. Working to create the mood was easier than I thought and it seemed so natural for them to be enveloped by my words and tonality. They responded without thinking too much, going with the flow, just letting their feelings emerge from within to produce a thinking photograph; what was in their heart and minds, a reflection of thought.

As you can see they are off center leading the viewer into the image from left to right and stopping them from travelling outside the image. We need to be satisfied with what we see before we completely leave a photograph. Perhaps it will linger in our thoughts and like a small seed may it grow and discover how we might photograph a similar scene. The work of others has had that kind of impact on me and I can see it in some of my work.

There is a circular movement around their faces and is slightly off colour. This was done intentionally as if influenced by a painter who took over for a split second, getting caught up in the moment and then back to some semblance of reality. On the left the chair adds a shape, a distance to feel the three dimensional reality. The background is an umber flavour often used by the old masters and darkened on the edges to help the viewer focus on the subjects. The purpose of this piece of art, as they saw the finished image, was to satisfy their wish. With complimentary words they took the image home, both emotionally and literally.

The influence of the old masters is so great that no one can escape their presence in all forms of art, no matter how far reaching that may be.

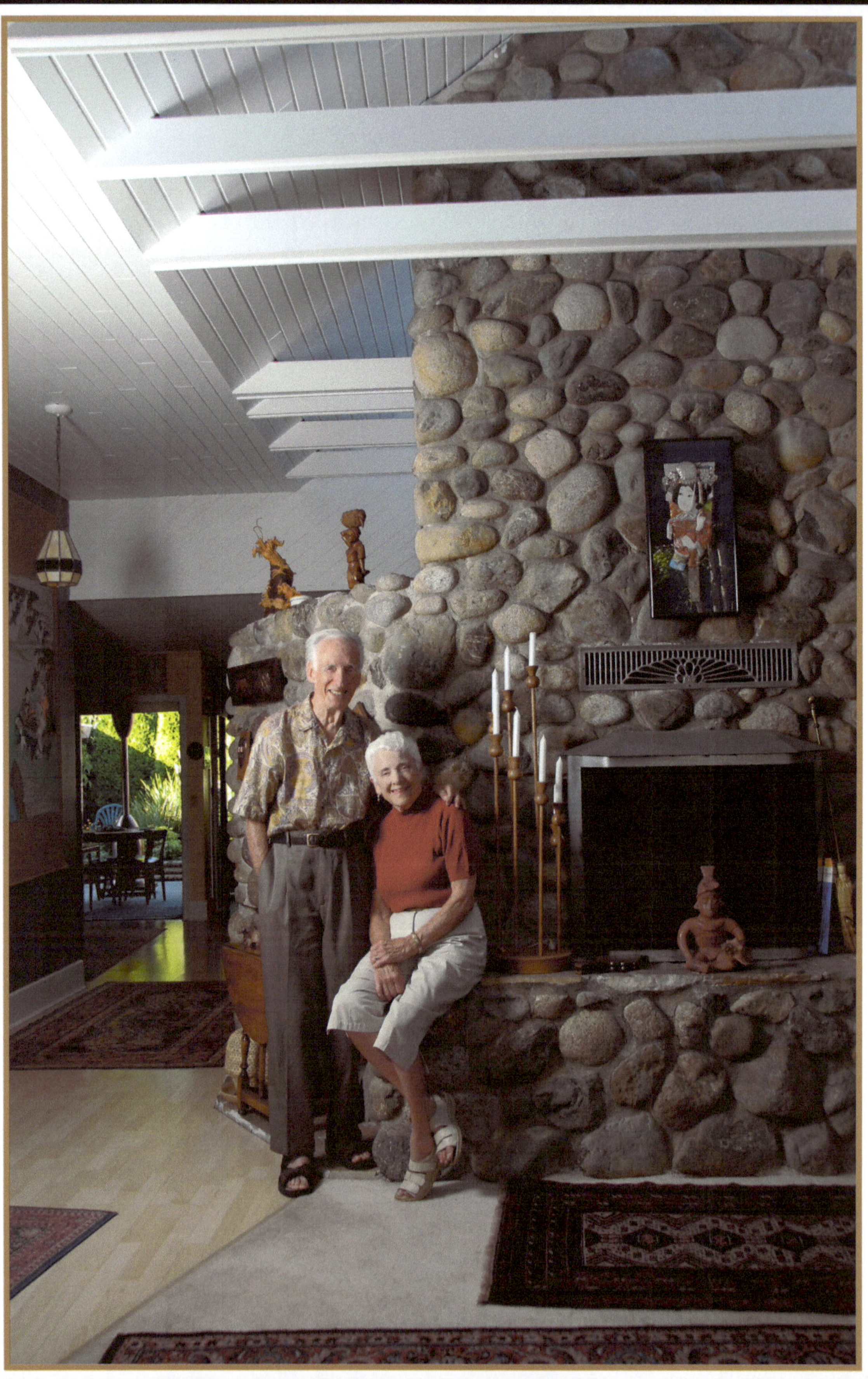

A Lifetime of Memories

I gave a gift certificate to our local Rotary Club in Victoria, British Columbia, as a goodwill gesture because I had been a Rotarian for many years in Saskatchewan. I received a phone call from the recipients of this certificate and they sounded very excited.

This older couple was full of life. The husband had worked in a photo lab in his younger years and knew a lot about photography. I was surprised when he said, "I didn't see the angle you set your camera up before but when you went out to get something I looked through your lens and recognized that you knew what you were doing."

They had a heritage home before purchasing their current house and spoke about the other home with fond memories. The reason they purchased this house was because it had all the rooms on one floor, whereas the heritage home had three floors and a long winding staircase. I found their new place to be very warm and cozy with easy access in every direction and had a vaulted ceiling. The angle I chose incorporated the living room with fireplace and the objects on and around the mantel had so much meaning because they collected these items from all over the world. The photograph extends down the short hall into their dining room and beyond onto the patio and garden outside. I love the depth and so did they. When we look into a portrait the feeling of depth that some photographers achieve always amazes me, which I also strive for when the opportunity arises.

Studying the image we can see how I had to have the camera in just the right place. I chose the camera position vertically but the horizontal plane also had a bearing on the image because if it was too high or too low it would distort the image. The position of the people determines a lot as to how we set up the camera. All the lighting was coming from a window or opened door but I enhanced the intensity with the halo soft box light I brought so the direction of the light would be obvious. This helped me to use the depth of field to my advantage so the viewer's eyes could enjoy the entire image and yet focus on the couple as the strongest point. If an image is razor sharp it can take away from the mood and feeling of the photograph. In this particular case the softness of the image as a whole emphasizes the mood and feeling portrayed by this lovely couple. The viewing distance and the overall size of the finished image beckon the clarity that is needed.

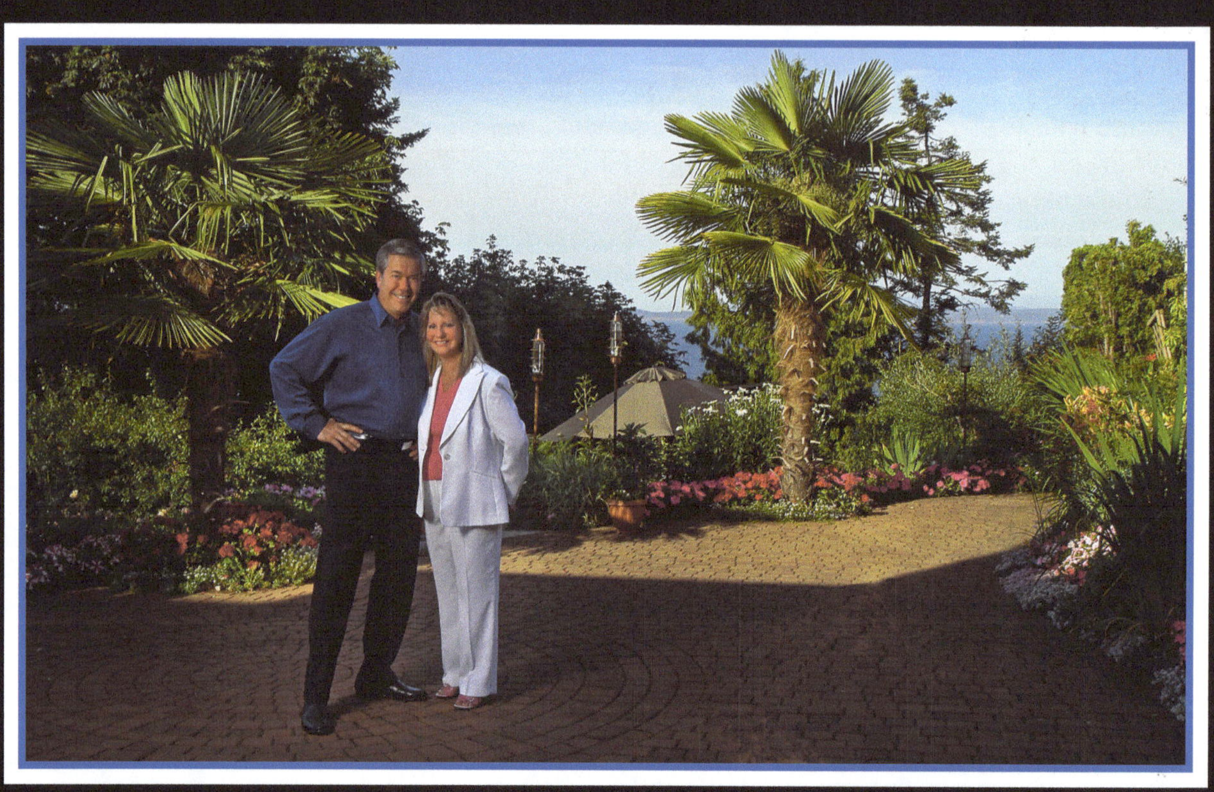

Simply the Best

These are long time friends and clients. He owns a high-end men's clothing store that I have frequented for many years, long before I moved to Victoria, so it was time for reciprocity. They posed in their huge backyard with its many layers. The view is breathtaking and in the distance you can see the Pacific Ocean and the snow capped Olympic Mountains of Washington State.

I love his store because it is the most outstanding clothing store in Victoria, perhaps even in all of British Columbia. Over the years I have purchased many ties, shirts, pants, etc. from him because it is always a treat to shop there. There's always something new, always something I like and nothing but the finest quality. I like to shop in a place where it is fun and the customer is well looked after.

When we had the consultation the main focus was on the location. I viewed their property earlier and suggested the area seen in the photograph. They liked this particular image so much that they purchased it as a 40-inch print on canvas. When someone sells clothing for a living you don't tell them what to wear however I did suggest the pose and captured their welcoming expressions. The composition worked well with the light and shadow on the brick, the V-shape and the trees added to the depth. By bringing them forward it is as if they are inviting you into the image.

Looking at the image we can of course see two people and when we study the environment there are also two palm trees and two lanterns. An inverted pyramid on the bricks formed by the sunlight forms an arrow back to the viewer and provides a unique composition that I had never created before. Wispy colours in the soft blue sky added so much depth we can almost walk right into the scene. The lines in the work print illustrate unique shapes added by the trees; think of the roundness on top of the trees because the trees were chosen with design in mind.

Their expressions are harmonized and yet their body language remains individualistic. The overall strength created by the stance and positioning of the two subjects adds variety to the study of composition.

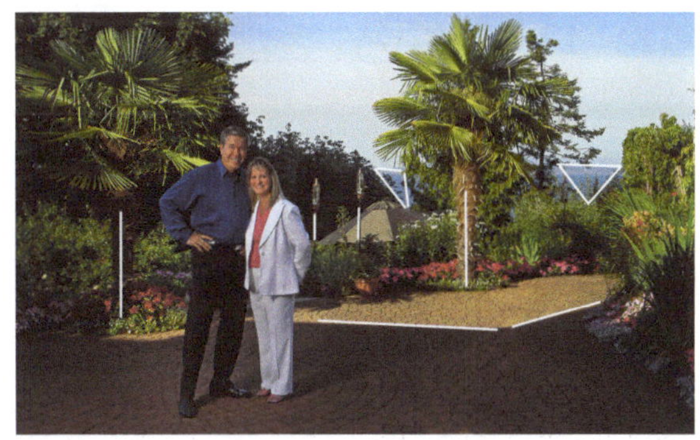

They are a warm and hospitable couple and are generous to a fault. When you want to enjoy the best you need to be with the best, purchase the best you can afford and be the best you can be.

This couple is simply the best!

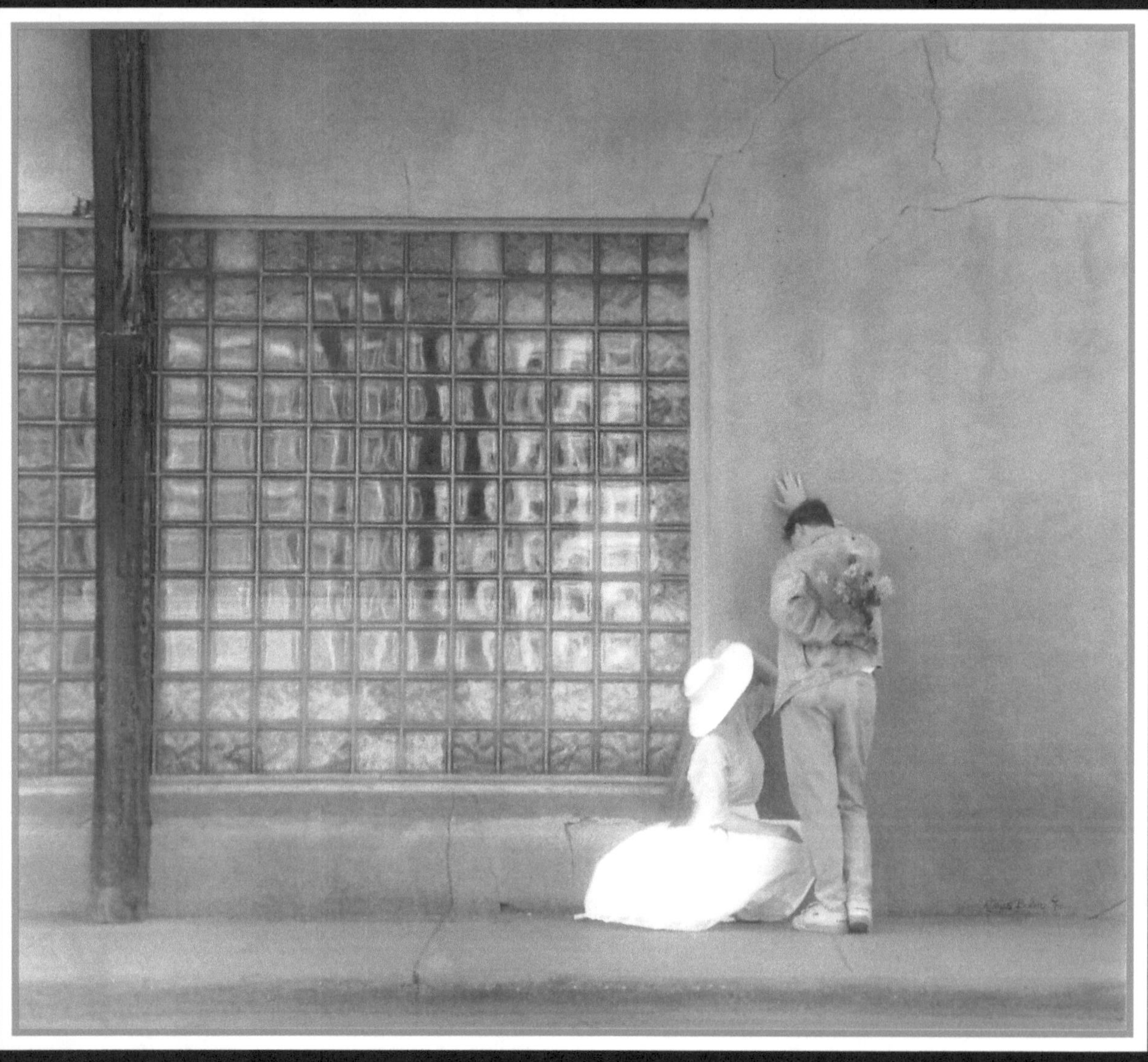

The Art of Love

This couple had me photograph their wedding one year earlier and asked me to photograph them on their anniversary. I was instructed to simply do whatever I wanted. All they asked was that it be an art piece and to finalize the image before revealing it. This image was to be unveiled for the first time at a large gathering of friends and family.

It came as a surprise because no one had asked me to do this before that point in time. Valuing the request and knowing that I needed to come up with a new dimension, it required that I stretch my creativity and come up with something that I had never done before. The location I used had been in the back of my mind for some time and I was hoping to use it when the subject matter was right. Now was the time.

I asked the couple to wear something similar to what they were wearing during our consultation: a dress for the wife, jeans for the husband and perhaps a prop like a hat and flowers. My suggestions were loose and non-restrictive, allowing them to choose the colour scheme. It was interesting because in my mind I wanted to show their faces and until then I had never sold a photograph without faces. I wanted to use this image for display so my clients could appreciate the art of photography.

Exploring the work print, the telephone pole on the left adds balance and strength to the overall image in the way it almost cuts the photograph from top to bottom. I like the blackness of the pole, this hybrid image, part colour part black and white needed strong design and impact that would challenge the viewer to think, look and read a message into it for themselves. The couple is separated from the pole by glass bricks which add to the overall design and rectangular shape. Take particular notice of the individual shape of each glass brick as they are square like the image but the image is not perfectly square. We added colour to a few of the glass bricks to echo the colours the couple is wearing. Notice the shape their bodies are forming and both sets of hands almost as if I placed them there myself. I guided their body language as a movie director would instruct actors and then allowed the subjects some leeway. Positioning the couple at the right hand thirds at the bottom allowed for a liberal use of space in the photograph thereby letting the cracked wall provide a little texture to the image.

The bodies are overlapped to show their union. The man is hiding the flowers as a gesture to his wife with his right knee bent as if to move in closer to her. She is kneeling and holding her hat to hide from the camera and reveal herself to him alone. Privacy, shyness and tenderness are expressed so completely, so touchingly. We all need to use our hearts to feel a photograph that can tell us a love story and yet remain untold in its entirety, hoping it will linger a little longer.

Yes the unveiling was a success for them, for me and their friends. May they be kept together by love and trust as a photograph, as a picture of happiness and an image to last and be spoken of far into the future. The art of love needs to be learned with practice of self discipline and new adventure in the days ahead; to learn to love more, to be more, to see more and to feel more deeply.

Returning to the work print again, we can see that balance can be created through illusion. The telephone pole on the left is visually much heavier because it is much closer to the left edge of the image but we can see that the couple placed close together brings everything back into balance. The glass bricks add to the balance because the fulcrum is at the 'V' immediately adjacent to the window and pole. We can imagine the pole going on forever without end or does it only extend beyond the edge of the photograph? The invisible eye lines are suggestive but through experience we believe it to be so.

Feel the image; the heart of the couple, playful, alone, flirting and yet we see no faces. The story is simply told through design and our own experiences.

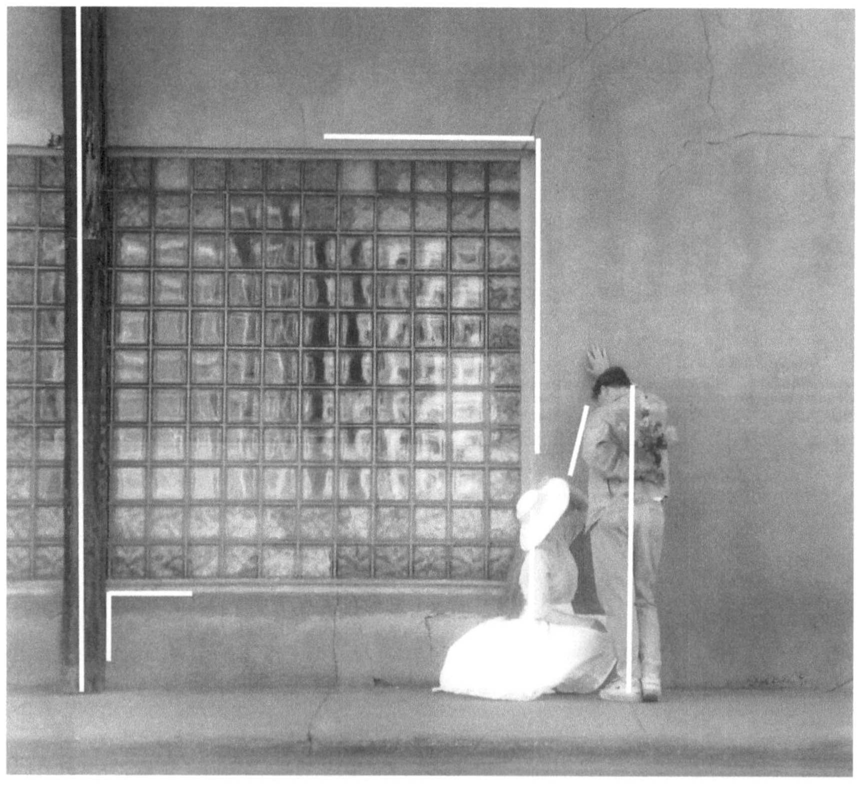

People and Pets

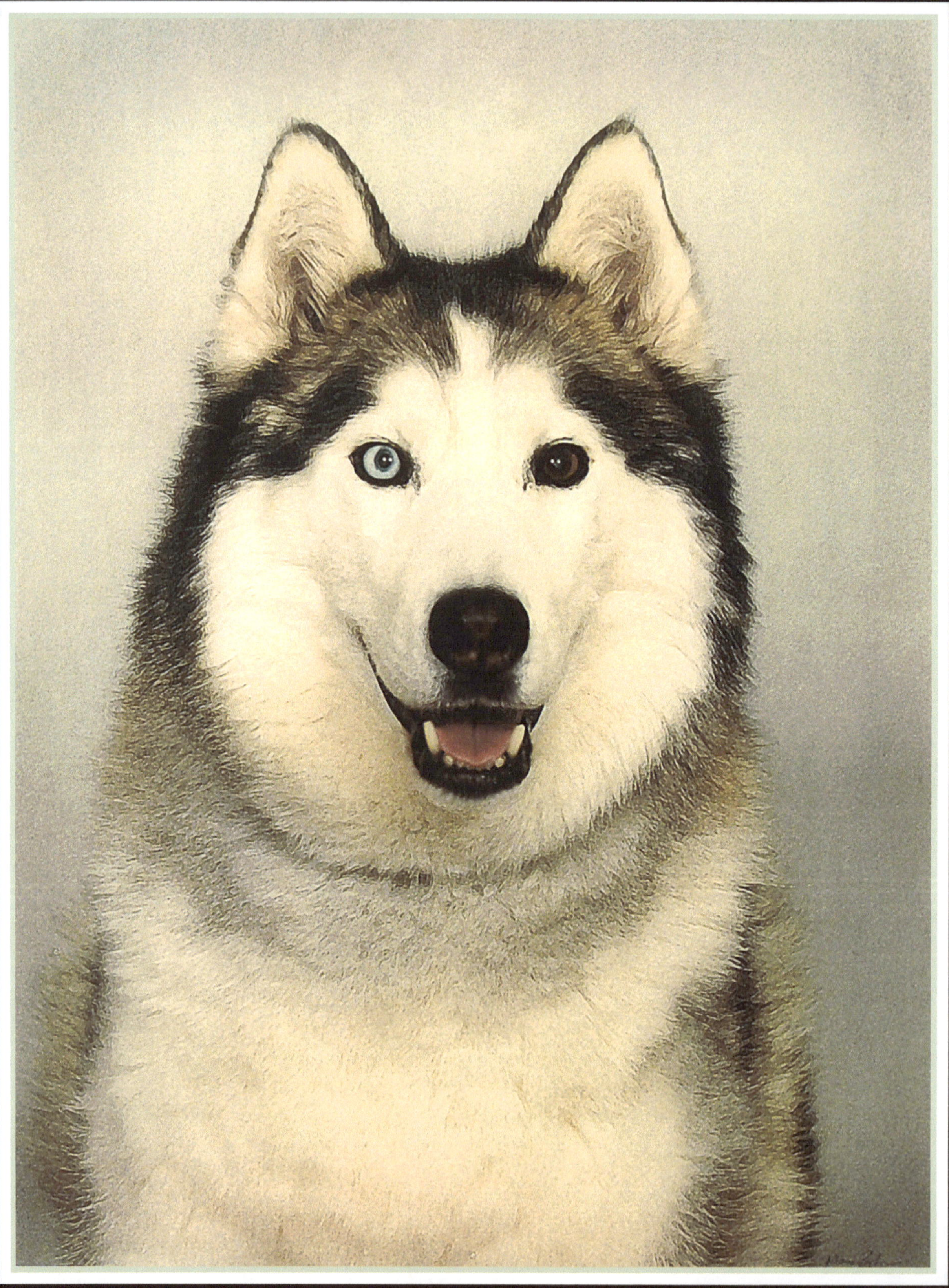

Man's Best Friend

This dog's owner accompanied her daughter-in-law and grandchild while they were picking up their watercolour portrait. She was impressed with the images and asked if I would photograph her dog, to which I immediately agreed. This fine award winning dog and his owner lived in Winnipeg, Manitoba. She had previously commissioned two paintings of her dog but felt that each time the artist failed to capture the dog's personality.

Some time later I unexpectedly received a phone call from this woman. She had driven with her dog all the way from Winnipeg to Vancouver, British Columbia. She was on the ferry coming to Victoria and asked when she could bring in the dog to be photographed. My response was, "Whenever you want!" The dog was older with some health problems and that was one of the reasons she drove instead of flying as she had indicated previously. He had a lovely face and gave me a smile when I made a noise with a squeaker to cause him to lift his ears and give me his full attention. He even sat up more and had a better posture. I like a smile on animals because they are not forced or unnatural.

The image presented in this book is the one she wanted and I told her that printing it on watercolour paper would give it a longer life. I used some filters to enhance its artistic look, especially with his two different coloured eyes. An overall texture was added but the tongue and eyes were left natural. He looks so perky and playful in the portrait, it's really a wonderful image.

Immediately upon receiving the photograph she called to tell me how impressed she was with the finished portrait and how I was able to capture the true essence and personality of her dog. The cost of transportation and the portrait were all worth it because of the resulting memory as well as an art piece to be passed down to the next generation.

Some time after this fine dog passed away she got a puppy somewhat similar to her first dog and of course I was asked when I could photograph this new addition to her family. He was young and playful and more difficult to settle down but nevertheless we were able to produce a watercolour in the same vein as the first image.

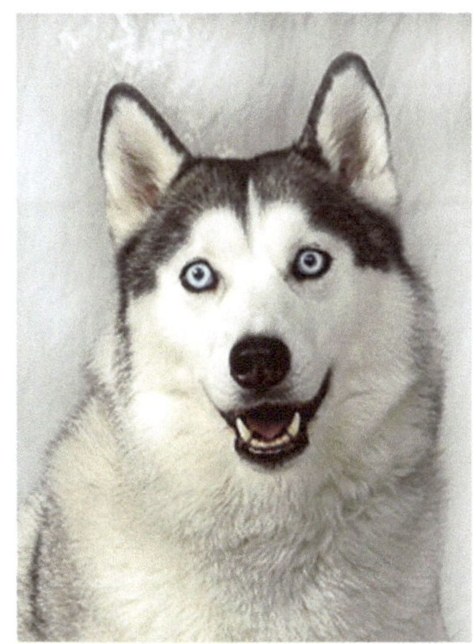

Oh how important pets can be to people. To learn from their undying love and contentment with people, especially their caregivers, knowing they belong and are loved in return. May we respect our animals as much as they respect us, with their love and kindness always waiting for us to come home and ready for us to take them for a walk even when we don't feel like it, and then feel better because we did.

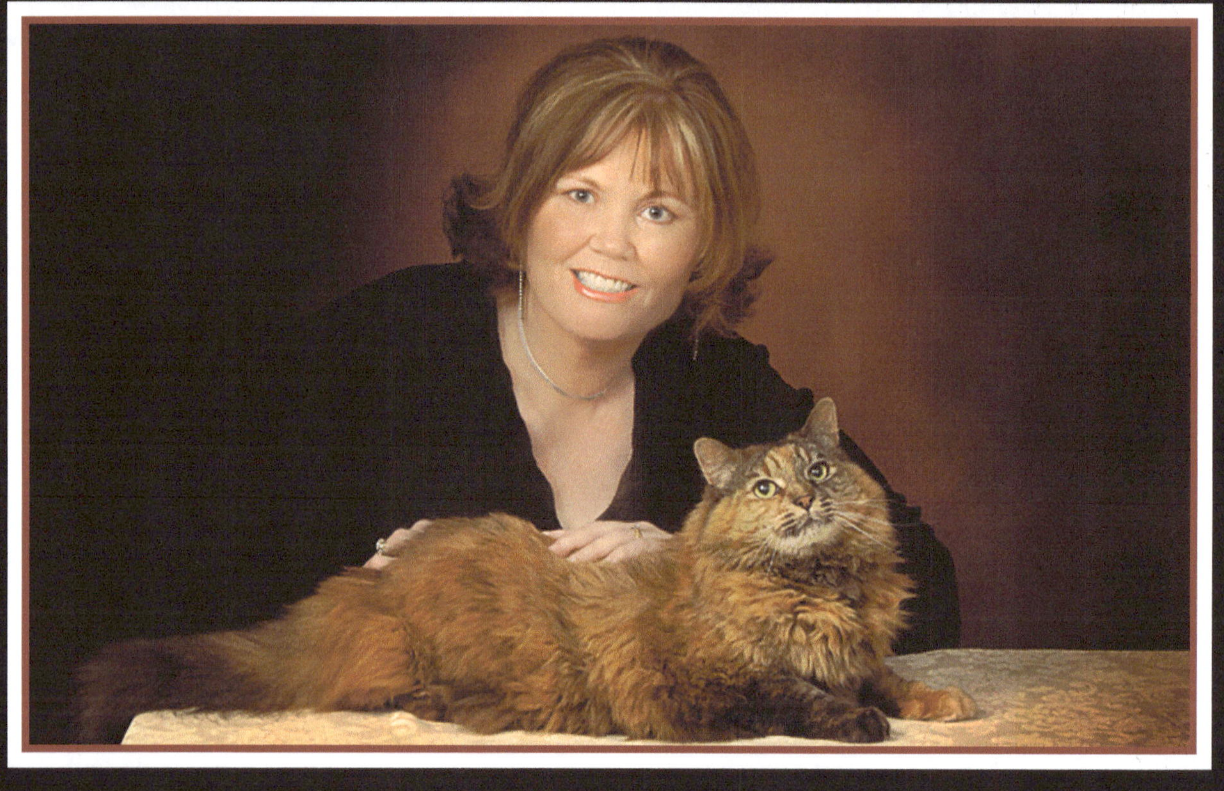

A Feline's Perspective

Cats are a species that I hadn't really studied or observed with interest in days past. Growing up on a farm cats were around in the barn but never in the house. They were always needed to keep the mouse population in check, to prevent them from over running the farm and house. Even on my own acreage we had cats for the same reason. I had to grasp that cats had individual personalities and unique qualities far beyond their natural function.

Moving to Vancouver Island I was introduced to the love of cats. So many people loved cats; not for their hunting ability but just for the love of cats. I had the privilege to photograph Jasmine Kinnear's wedding and a couple years later I was commissioned to photograph cats for her book cover. I did some research by reading one of Jasmine's books. I learned that cats communicate using different vocalizations. We need to hear and differentiate between the different sounds and respond in kind or at least know their needs and wants. As I discovered from my daughter Tammy's cat they can be rather demanding. She asked, "Dad, can you look after my cat while I'm away? It's just for a little while and then I'll take Betty home again." Needless to say, that has happened a few times now because she is a flight attendant and is on the road, so to speak, for long stretches of time. She works out of Calgary but moved to Victoria to spend more time with me and our whole family. Well I may be stuck with her cat but that's a small price to pay to have Tammy close to home.

How interesting this cat became to me, her personality was so engaging I couldn't help but respond with strokes of kindness and we were soon fast friends. I learned her routine. For example, if I was in the kitchen and she looked up to the top of the fridge it meant that she wanted her treat because that is where I keep her treats. No meows, just a look; she sits like a puppy looking up, not begging, just demanding her rights. In the morning or at dinner time it is quite different. She meows as a command, "Feed me now!" "Meow, meow, meow," and so on as if I did not hear her because she is impatient. It is as if she is saying, "This is my right, and I want it right now!" There is so much we learn from each other.

The photographic session was done in stages. Jasmine arrived first with the props and then her husband arrived shortly thereafter with the cats. There wasn't just one, but four and I must admit that at times it seemed like there were seven. They all wanted to explore the camera room and beyond but were restricted because we closed all the doors. In and out of hiding places, food and water was set up for them and a litter box too. My studio was no longer mine as the cats literally took over. However I must say that when it was all over I could look back and say it was fun. The passion of the cat handler and the model was helpful and energizing. In time we captured what was needed for their purpose; the cat looking up with expectation and interest, wanting to be entertained but with a very short attention span. It took a lot of effort from everyone present to make the photo look so at ease and comfortable. Thanks to digital photography there was no lack of shots during this session.

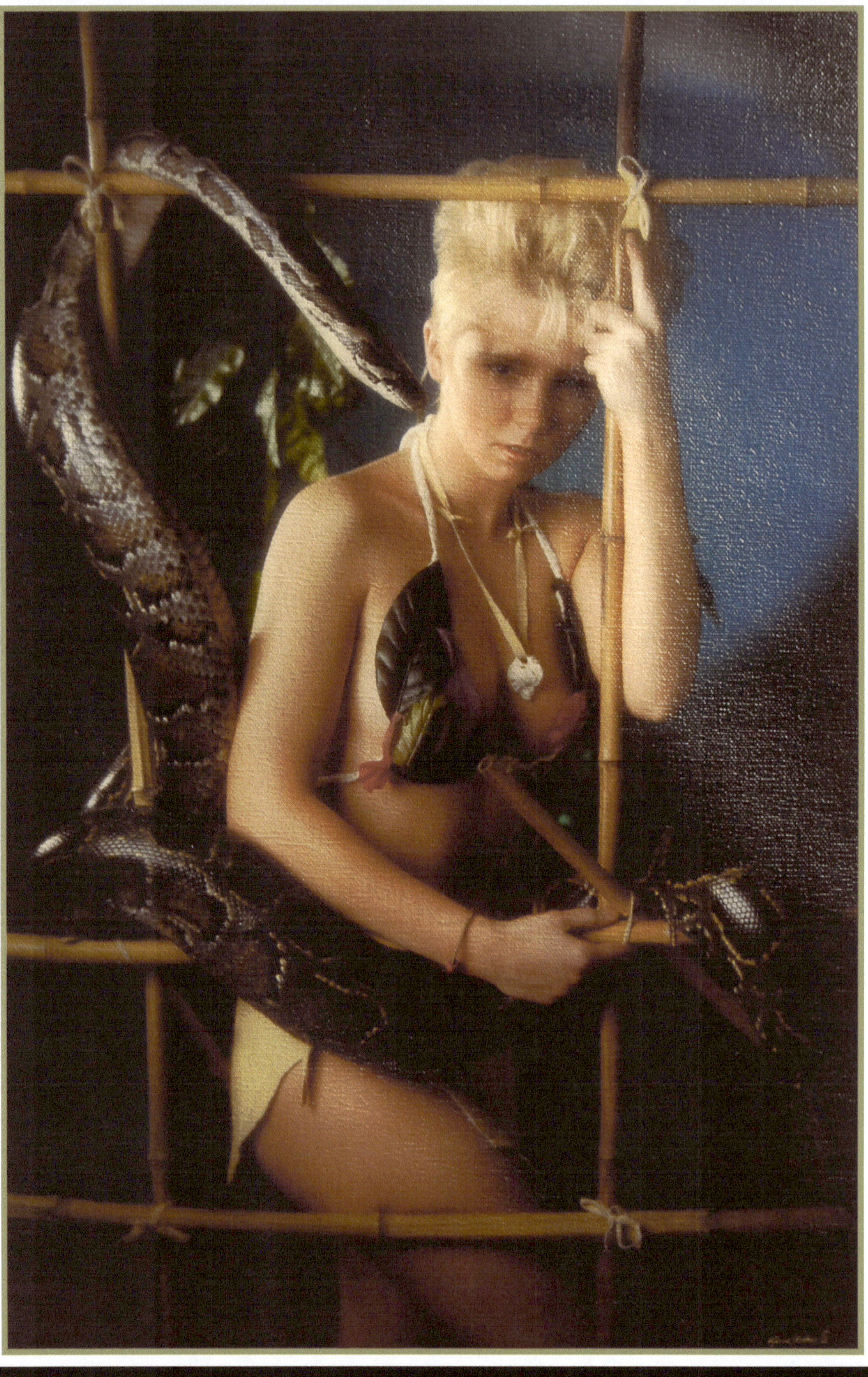

Temptation

When we look at art created centuries ago the Biblical influence is so apparent: Eve with the apple and Eve with the snake of temptation. I have photographed both of these impressions left to us by artists and painters of the past and we have been influenced so dramatically that we believe in the concept that these artists have given us.

I received a long distance phone call from a young lady in Edmonton, Alberta. She wanted to have photographs taken by me because she heard that I was a good photographer. In particular she wanted to know how I could photograph her in such a way that modelling agencies or whomever she would give her photos to would always remember her. I blurted out that she should rent a snake. There was silence for a moment and then she told me she would call me back. The next day she set up an appointment with me for the following week.

There they were the model, the snake and the snake handler. I could hardly believe it myself. How did I come up with the snake? I guess seeing the photo by Richard Avedon (1923-2004) of Nastassja Kinski and the Serpent made such a profound impression on me that I kept it in the back of my mind and when I needed inspiration the image came to the forefront. This happens to me quite frequently. I log away impressions, keep them handy and get inspired in times of need. Don't just copy, do not copy. If you just copy you will have weakened your opinion of yourself, degraded and harmed any creativity you might have had. Positive self appreciation can only inspire and motivate our growth.

When we started to assemble a simple set and introduce the model into the set I had to get ready with my lighting, camera and concept, and then bring in the boa constrictor. The snake didn't cooperate. I knew that somehow we would not only have to keep the model looking sombre and seduced but also allow the snake to twist and curve its way to *Eve's* head. I noticed that the snake liked hair. Perhaps it was the warmth from her head? So with this in mind we were able to guide the snake by placing the model in just the right position to *tempt* the snake. Oh what a twisted *tail* we weave in our photographs when a story is in the making.

While studying the photograph, the lines and angles, keep in mind the story and what this image is representing to the viewer who can read it without bias or judgement; just enjoying the story, the passion, the art, the conclusion derived by our mind, the finishing touch.

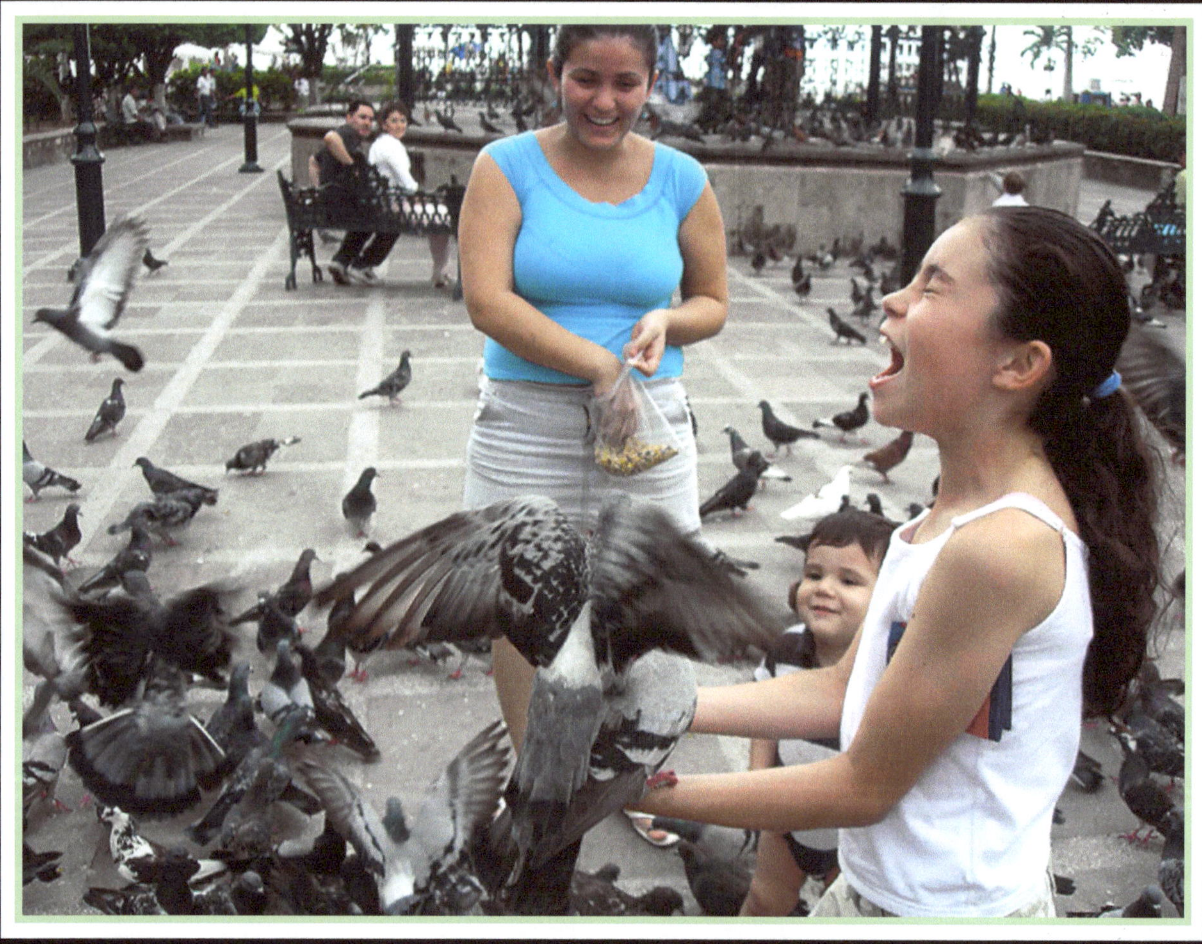

Wings in Flight

While in Mexico I liked watching birds and how they interacted with people, especially when there was food around. There is food for the body but let us also seek food for the mind! My anticipation paid off as I knew it would. I remember being in London's Trafalgar Square and running into the pigeons so they would scatter in flight. I made a print of this image of flying pigeons on paper I handcrafted myself and it's one of my favourite images from that trip. I always wanted to repeat this experience in a photograph with people in the image.

I suppose because we can't fly like birds, man has always sought to fly. Michelangelo drew pictures of flying machines and some even resembled helicopters. The ability to see from above, from the sky, from the heavens sparks our imagination and vision. Do you remember the first time you went up in an airplane, the excitement and how scary it was? I had the privilege to fly with the Snowbirds, an acrobatic flying team and Canadian icon comprised of serving members of the Canadian Forces. The effect of flying so fast and the G-forces we pulled turned my stomach, an experience I will not soon forget.

Birds and most animals have an innate force for survival, an instinct that is hewn by nature itself. Human nature drives man further, higher, longer and deeper because of our imagination. Food for thought is part of our lives and without this food we would live a very miniscule life, perhaps feeling unimportant just existing for a time without contributing to society, a meaningless life. This food which perhaps comes from above, the universal mind, where all knowledge exists from the past, present and future may have allowed Michelangelo to imagine a helicopter some six hundred years ago.

I like the little girl's reaction to the pigeons landing on her as she offered them food. Not just any food but food that the birds longed for and had an appetite for. It must have been both scary and fun for her to say the least. Look at the reaction not only of the little girl but I presume her mother and little brother, as well as the couple in the background sitting together like lovers. Life seeks thrills, excitement and new experiences as we live and more importantly become alive with far reaching experiences, unrehearsed, unexpected and with an unassuming attitude.

May we have this child-like curiosity so that life doesn't prevent each one of us from experiencing a full, rich, productive and adventurous life not measured by years but by experiences.

This may be a non-traditional format for a portrait but it has the ingredients and a mix of feeling, joy, movement, depth and curiosity which can only be measured in a portrait.

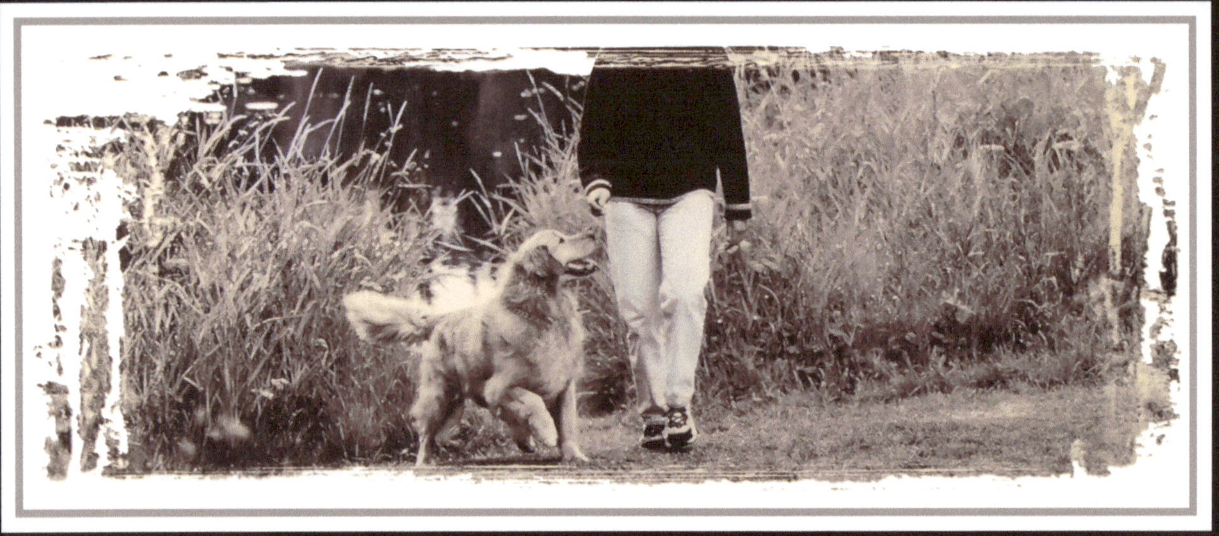

My Dog and I

When I had the consultation with this young woman it was evident that the dog was a very big part of her life and the emphasis needed to be on the dog. He was a fun loving dog and like so many pets they have a purpose to make us love them back in an unexplainable way. We chose the outdoors because they would often go for walks in this place; it was familiar and the dog was so content to be there and have fun. I hardly existed as far as he was concerned and that was just what I wanted.

I explored the photographs and started to see the possibilities: cropping, printing on watercolour paper and visualizing a panel shape. It may be easier to take in an image with this kind of format because we are used to movie screens in theatres and the format of new televisions and computer monitors. Since our eyes are side by side we see so much more horizontally than vertically. Whenever possible I prefer using the so-called landscape format because it can be soothing and peaceful as in this image.

The relationship these two have is evident in the expression on the dog's face: pure happiness. There was no need for me to include the woman's face because what the dog was saying in his body language and facial expression could not be improved upon. I cropped the photograph because we need to be careful not to compete for the viewer's attention or distract from a strong look that says too much.

I like the movement of the dog curling around his mistress in a loving way. All that was important to the dog was the one he knew and wanted to be with. The body of the young lady shows us movement in a straight line as she chooses the direction and is still in control. This dog is mesmerized by his beloved owner and wants to be close and in sync at all times.

Looking at the work print on the next page, the lines can help us see what is and what can be when we allow the subject free rein and the photographer waits for the right moment, also known as the decisive moment. French photographer Henri Cartier-Bresson (1908-2004) pioneered the art of street photography and his image *Behind the Gare St. Lazare, Paris* is the epitome of the term the decisive moment.

Expectation, anticipation, waiting for the right moment and thinking ahead; so often as photographers we are impatient and premature when it comes to pushing the button on the camera. In another book I will show more of this kind of photography: waiting patiently and reading the situation, allowing our intuition to rule.

Study the old master photographers because they will open your eyes to the birth of photography. We sometimes take for granted and have no understanding where things originated. If we don't understand the past we may lack understanding or display ignorance. In all other disciplines the past is well known to the practitioner. Would there be a qualified physician who didn't know the doctor who performed the world's first successful human-to-human heart transplant was South African cardiac surgeon Christiaan Neethling Barnard (1922-2001)?

One should study and love to study and learn not only with and through the camera but from books and lectures from notable individuals who have paid the price of learning and perhaps have talent to boot. Let us never stop learning because there is no end and there is no greater joy than to discover a secret that is revealed to us through learning.

Walking in step, in harmony, is so natural with most animals we do it unconsciously, it just happens; no extra effort is needed, let it happen. The dog's movement is in keeping with hers, how wonderful! Study the work print below and see the lines. Their combined motion, the emotion on the dog's face, do we need to say more? Learn to see the lines in a photograph as I have said before, make it happen.

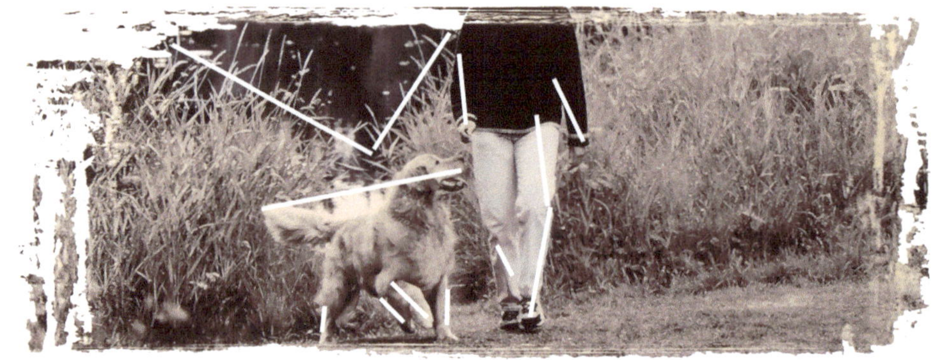

Music and Dance

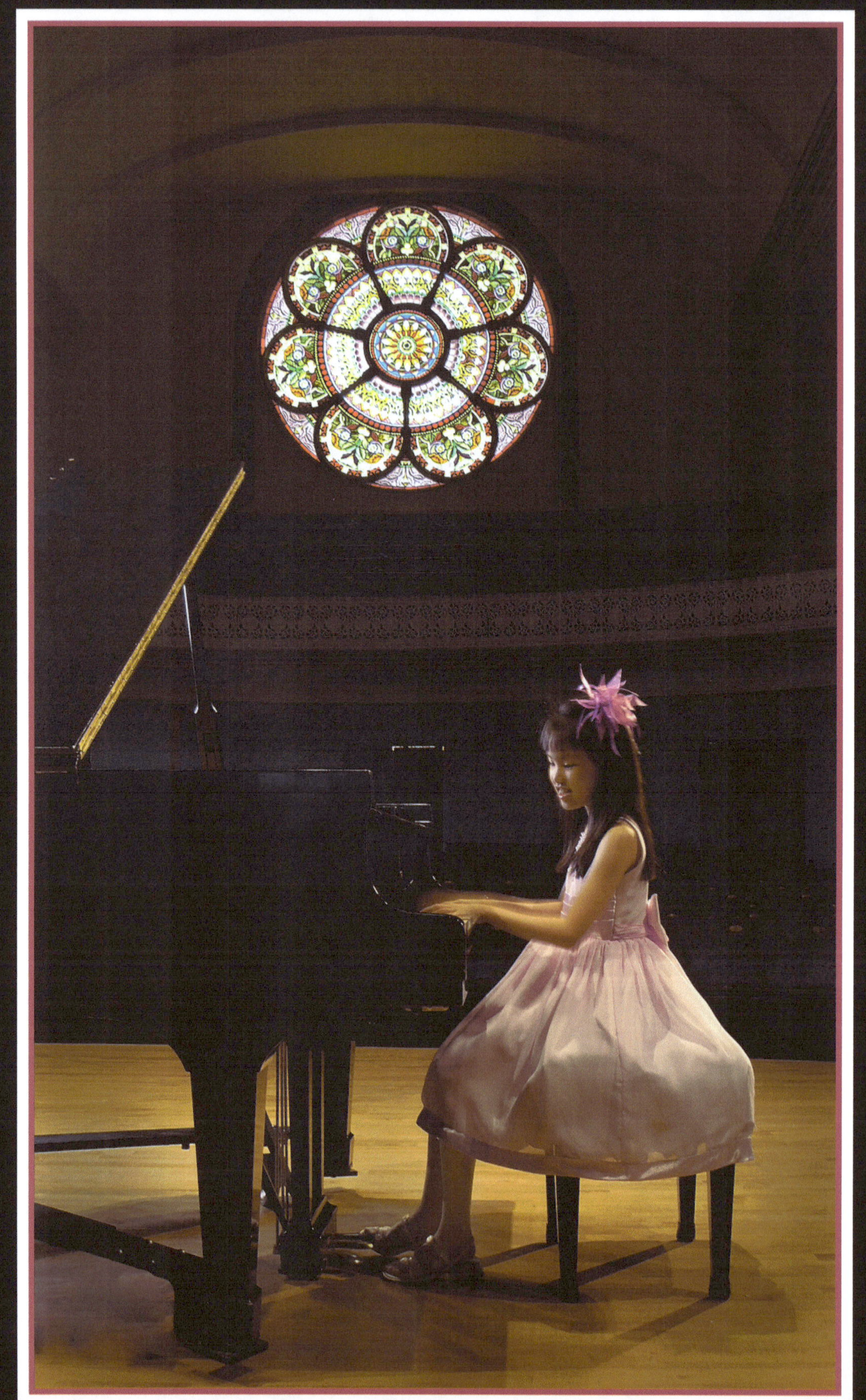

Piano Recital

So small and yet such a great talent, what wonders lie within the human body and mind. It is incomprehensible. How is it that sometimes we experience wonders beyond belief? What must it be like to be a little girl with a big piano in such a large space which can be filled with sound ringing throughout this vast cathedral? What joy it brings to her parents' hearts, filled with love and pride and so it should be. The accolades heaped on this very young pianist are surely well deserved.

Practice, practice and more practice. What does ongoing practice without genuine talent produce? All the practice in the world would not – could not produce a musician and not just an ordinary musician but a super star, a musician among musicians.

We are all formed with what we are given and our wants and desires cannot change the components we are made of. Yes, being dedicated can enhance our ability to a minor degree but only inborn talent can supersede all the practice and dedication we as humans can engage in.

Envy, jealousy and tears will not change who we are and what we can produce and share with others. It is not only sharing but the yearning, the need to produce. This powerful drive from within must be expressed even if just for ourselves before it bursts out uncontrollably, sweeter than fleshly pleasure. It is an unspeakable joy that no words can explain; my heart begs for definition but is simply unexplainable. However there are joyous thoughts that tread like angels amongst us.

We may encourage many while others we offer a word in season, in timely fashion, a touch of praise or applause. This gift is not overlooked; it is cherished by those who can and will appreciate it. May we have the courage to hold up the hands of the gifted as a sign of appreciation, not in selfishness, or regret or with feelings of inferiority but in *love*.

The composition of this image has components to help see beyond the obvious; the little girl sitting all alone at the piano as we may expect at a recital with her fingers nothing but a blur as she plays her heart out. Now study the rest of the photograph looking up to see the glass stained window, a symbol of unearthly light and imagery, a crowning glory of one who is so blessed with heavenly talent. Its circular design brings the eye back to the key, the subject. Even the lid of the piano influences the design as does the placement of the subject in the bottom right third. Learning to see composition is not an accident but rather we learn by practicing. Study the work of others, especially painters and even sculptors, to get a feeling for design and then use this emotion to fulfill our desire so that we may communicate and speak our mind using photography.

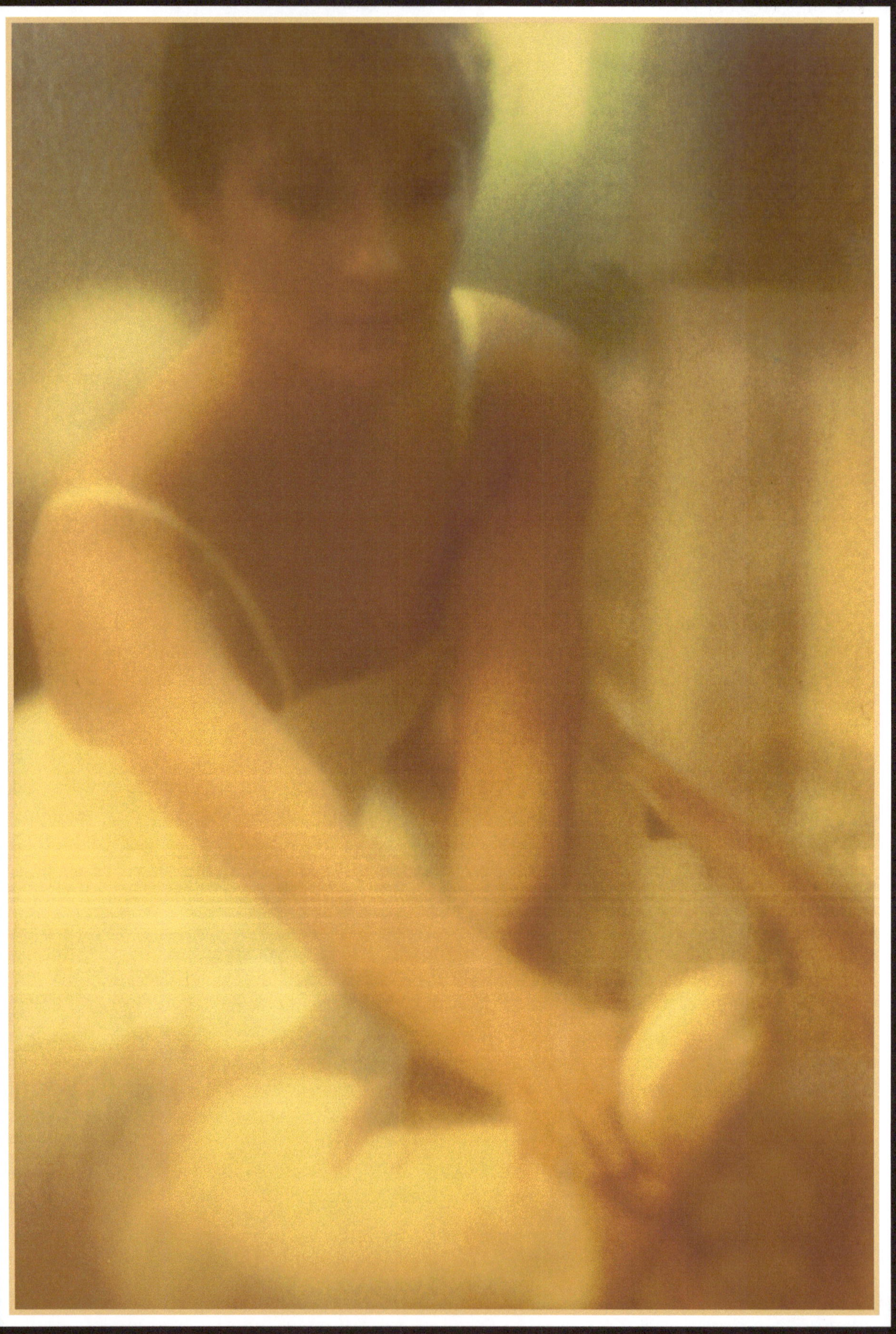

The Ballet Dancer

This was an image I had in mind for quite some time and then one day the opportunity came my way. As often happens if we think about something long enough, just waiting for the opportunity, it will present itself in time. I would like to give you a brief feeling of what draws me to impressionism, even in photography.

In 1883 the French poet Jules Laforgue (1860-1887) wrote, “The Impressionist eye is, in short, the most advanced eye in human evolution, the one which until now has grasped and rendered the most complicated combinations of nuances known.” Monet is one of the most well known impressionist artists who advocated this discipline in his work and life.

In the late 1860s, Claude Monet (1840-1926), Pierre-Auguste Renoir (1841-1919) and others painted in a new style, referred to as Impressionism by their contemporaries. Monet’s canvas entitled “Impression: Sunrise” (1873) best typifies this style. Originally it was intended to be a derogatory if not downright scandalous title for the non-traditional style. The Brushwork and images of the Impressionist was a revolutionary approach – reflective of those revolutionary times! From the use of light, colour and texture it is artistic imagery.

The Impressionism style is a worthy counterpoint to the realism of artistic modern photographers.

I love photographing dancers because they put their all into their art. They make the perfect pose, working so hard to become the best, the best they can be and the best that there is. I feel for their pain in practice and maybe even more so in their performance.

This was a great opportunity to work in the studio of a very well respected teacher with a student who she felt was able to perform her part so well. I used slide film with a 1600 ASA speed to provide texture and then over the lens I used a black chiffon cloth, the kind that is found in a loosely weaved lady’s scarf. These two elements added a softness and a haze over the entire image; the feeling and design is so apparent from the cool blue suggested by the window that it creates a feeling of depth. We can observe the turning of her shoulders in conjunction to the bar where dancers practice their stretches and warm ups. Her leg on the diagonal running along and resting on the bar gives focus to the image and a sense of the dancer’s need for perfection. Cropping into her head forces the viewer to look at the hands and feet, the ultimate because I heard instructors continually correcting the positioning of the hands, feet, head and shoulders. Her eyes are blurred giving meaning to the concentration that is so critical in this discipline and in the background out of focus we hardly recognize but can imagine another dancer practicing. The subject is completely inside herself so as not to be distracted in any way by outside forces, a discipline I can envy because it is so necessary in photography as well.

The impression is all that we can carry with us, in whatever form we can capture in our mind and savour it in our hearts. There are many images that have left me in awe. They can still be seen clearly in my thoughts and I carry them with me in my heart because the imprint then became permanent. How these hauntingly beautiful images have perpetually influenced my work and have no doubt even enhanced my latest work.

By studying the work print below we can see all the lines lead to the dancer's foot. I learned a profound lesson: if a dancer's feet don't have what it takes then it doesn't matter how much she wants it because it just will not happen.

I wanted the emphasis to be where it counts, the foundation. When we study ballet or simply watch a performance we can appreciate their feet. The price a dancer pays in pain and practice is not quantifiable; without gifted feet there is no hope. Of course let us not forget the hands, mind, back and so on which all enter into the equation to complete the dance.

I believe most of us have the ability to see lines and can begin to understand how to accomplish our purpose in life and achieve results. British born photographer David Hamilton is well known for pioneering the "soft-focus" style. His technique gives many of his works the appearance of an impressionist oil painting versus a true-to-life crisp photographic image. He photographs in a dreamy, romantic, and tranquil style, characterized by subdued natural lighting, graceful period clothing of muted pastel hues, lace and flowers. I have appreciated David Hamilton's work and how he uses different techniques to produce extraordinary images, such as adding Vaseline or hair spray to a filter to achieve his end result. May we study and discover new artistic freedoms in his profound work.

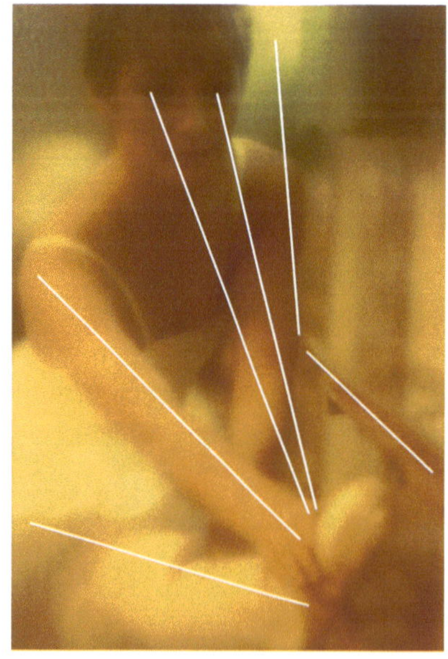

"A photograph is usually looked at -
seldom looked into."
-Ansel Adams

"To love what we do and cherish the results
of our labour is an unspeakable joy
and fills us full of bliss."
-Klaus Bohn

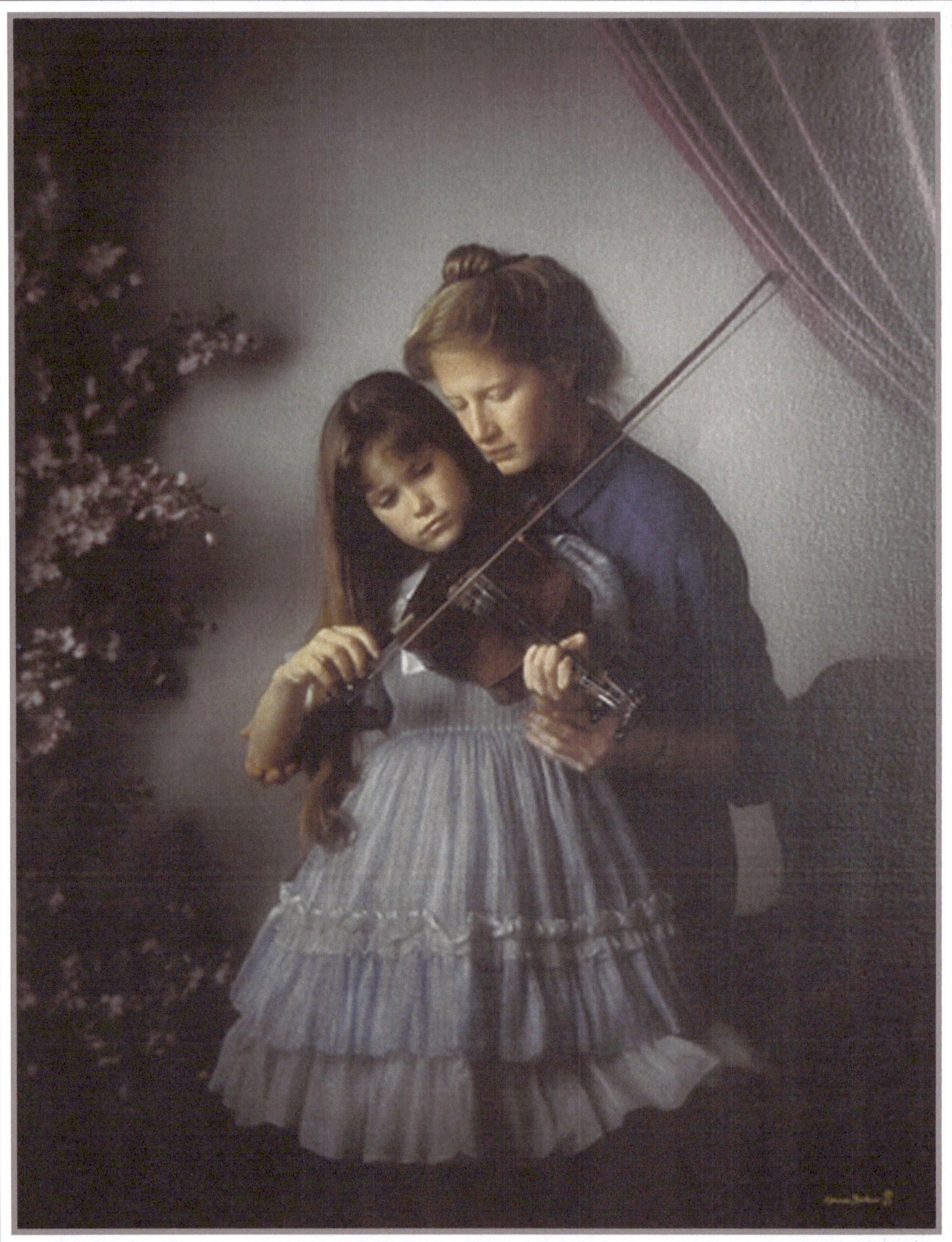

The Music Lesson

When my daughter Tammy wanted to take music lessons we wondered which instrument it would be. We gave her suggestions but a friend of ours played the violin, so she thought that this would be cool. Unlike her bother Michael who barely completed one piano lesson, perhaps this would be a better choice for her. I had my doubts but for once I kept them to myself! Her other brother David never took music lessons when he was small and yet today he plays the guitar and has a drum set too.

I needed to record this monumental step for my little girl. Will she perform on stage around the world? Little do we know what the future holds but dreams are there to indulge our fantasies and they prepare us for what awaits us. When I started my studio business I made a poster that read, “Think Big.” Of course it had to do with purchasing large photographs but *dream big* is its equivalent. I would never want to say what our forefathers might have said about being realistic; what crippling words for a child, how damaging.

I photographed Tammy and made it look more professional by having her hold the violin. At the time I took this photograph she had not even had her first lesson. Setting the stage with curtains, props, clothing and hair all give the image authenticity, looking as though the first lesson had just begun. The intensity of expression, the gentleness of the instructor, fitting it all together became a challenge in itself.

Where to look? It seems that whenever there is a camera present everyone expects to look at the lens. My question is why? Who came up with this idea? Surely it was not the painters, so please allow me to shed some light on this conditioning. We need to return to the olden days way back at the beginning... I don’t mean creation or the big bang theory but the beginning of photography. The exposure of the first photograph was hours in the making and as photography improved the length of the exposure improved dramatically to just 10 minutes more or less. Braces were used to clamp the neck to reduce movement during the long exposure. The subject needed to sit and hold still by looking at the camera. This is how it became known to have a sitting. The person focused their eyes on the lens and this would remind them not to move. Then in later years Hollywood came on the scene. Not only was looking at the camera a must but also a big smile from ear to ear, I suppose to indicate how wonderful movie stars’ lives are, full of luxury and fame.

We need to realize that the painter or artist seldom worked this way. If we are to learn from the great ones who came before us, may I suggest not to instruct people to look at the camera and say, “On three... one, two, and three!” Taking a picture in this manner is not making a photograph. As I have said many times, “If I ever ask someone to smile I will give them all their photographs for free!” I never use the words smile, fuzzy pickles, cheese, stinky socks, sex, whisky, frisky, peanut butter, Wayne Gretzky and so many others that I have heard.

The subject needs to be involved in whatever they are doing and it needs to be believable because it is real at least in that split second of time. Let's tell the truth as we see it in just that moment. Even in a make believe world there can be believability for the dreamer.

Music, sound, purpose, feeling and touch all resonate from this image. We know this from experience; maybe not the reality of playing an instrument or even a violin in particular but we have heard and experienced sound and music in abundance.

Looking at the work print image with circles and a pyramid, the sound flows out like a ring similar to throwing a pebble in the water. I designed the image with this thought in mind, at least intuitively. The strength of the pyramid, an often used symbol, is something we can relate to as the great pyramids of Egypt have been standing for centuries. We mounted the photograph on canvas thereby adding texture and an impression from art of old.

Examining the overall impact, the storytelling and communication not only from the author of the image but also the subjects within the image, we see them playing their roles like a movie with only one frame because more is not needed. I believe that we tend to make photographs too complex, trying to say too much, too loudly, too simply, too long, too short and so on. We need to learn to say it right, nothing more and nothing less. Just right!

A certificate of authenticity was made to add emphasis to the canvas, thereby allowing the viewer to know who made the image and the subjects within the photograph. We are accustomed to just looking at an image without giving too much consideration to the author of the photograph. I heard Edward Weston's son speak in Calgary, Alberta, a number of years ago. I purchased a student print of the image *Pepper No. 40* because it was affordable at that time. The image was Mr. Weston's (1886-1958) and even though he didn't print it himself, the image was still his and I have it hanging proudly in my home. Even if there are those who copied his image in their own way, there is only one *Pepper No. 40*. A student may have printed it and perhaps retouched it but the image still belongs to its creator.

I sometimes present a certificate of authenticity with my finished work to help owners and those who may later study the images value the work more. By knowing who took the photograph it helps the viewer to really see the image, know the image and understand the image. As we study and learn in this way, with time may we all be "feeling more deeply about photography."

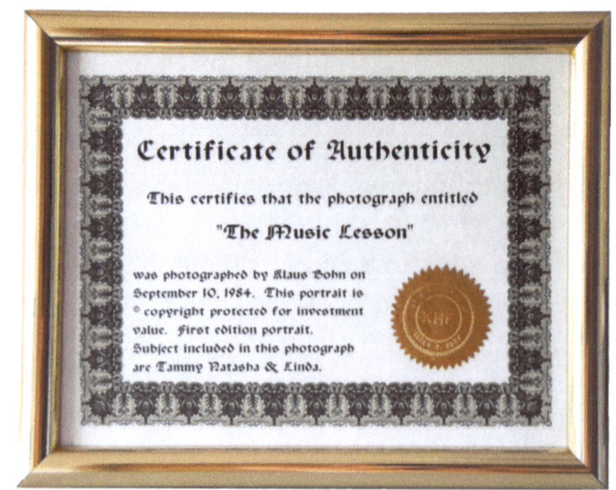

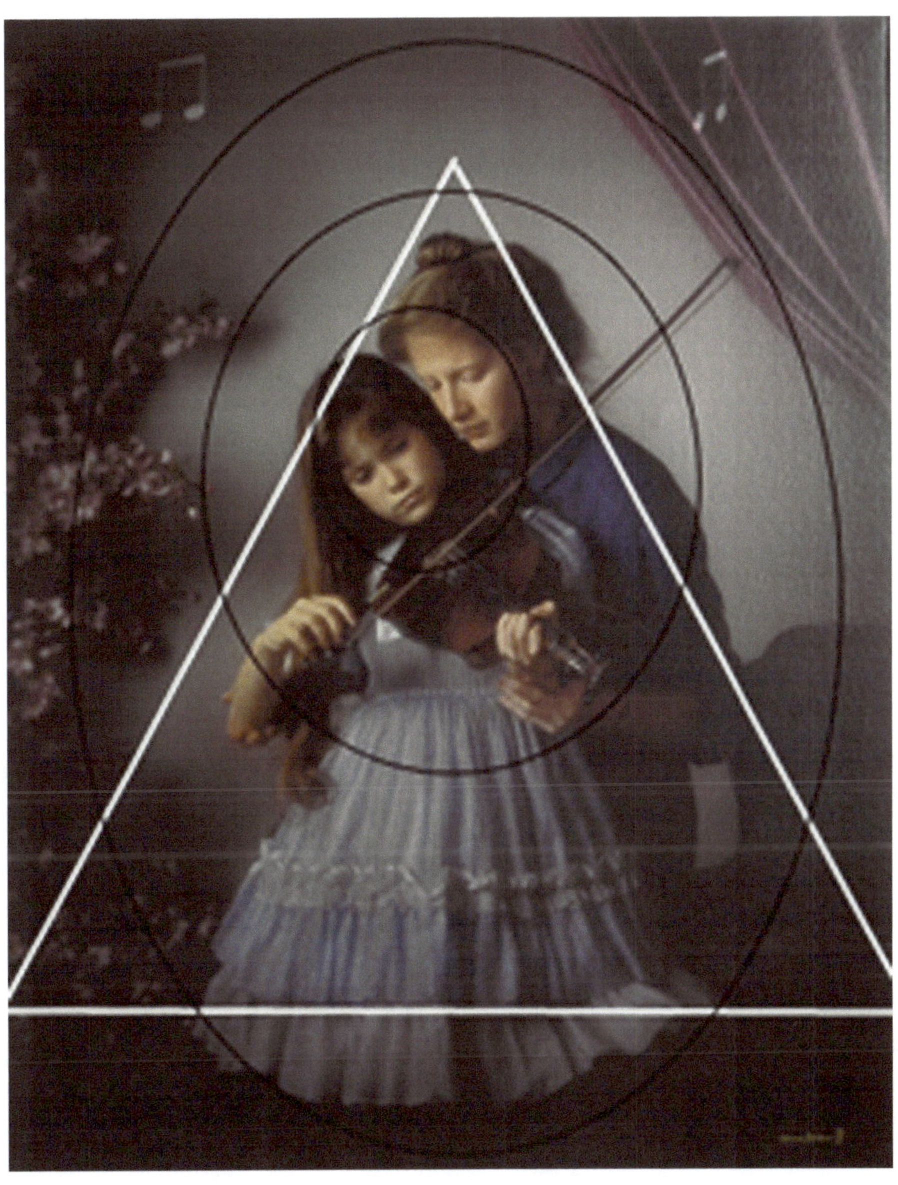

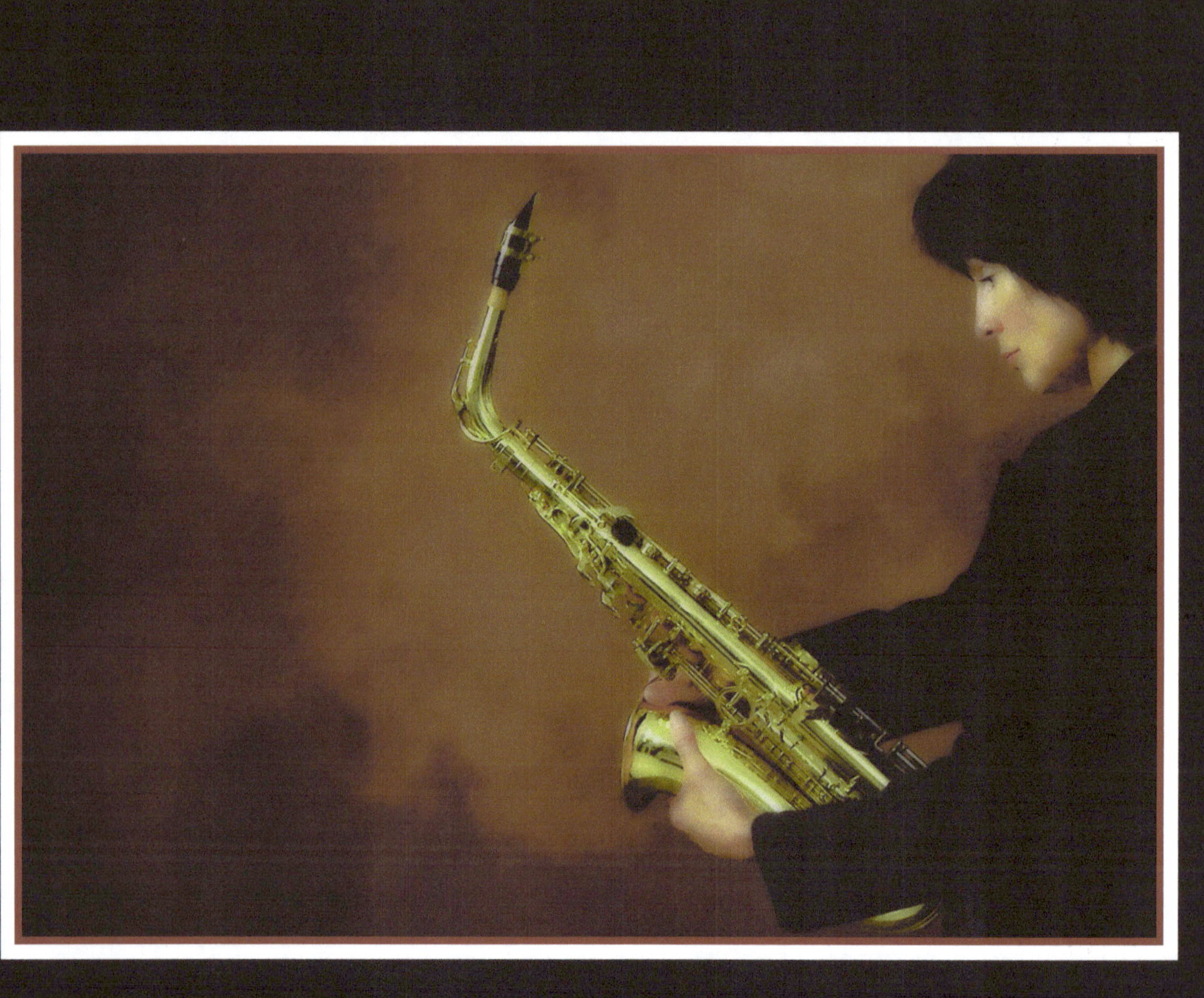

Space

If space is infinite, why are we as photographers so shy in expressing it? Do we have to play the instrument in order to hear the music? Many such questions are on the tip of our tongues but never asked.

Let us explore space for a moment. Why do we feel the need to crowd every image, make the viewer feel claustrophobic and unrealistically squish the subject into a tight space out of proportion? Can we value an image that is too small? We can house small photos easier and then they become record keepers which is valuable in that sense so as to recall the event.

To produce an art piece we need to explore the space we have to work with, the size of the paper, canvas, wood, etc. and the subject matter. All these things must be taken into consideration as well as the artists' own impression and that which they want to leave behind.

Sound is something we can hear through our ears or just feel the music and hear it in our mind. There is also the sound of silence. Just seeing an instrument can change our mood and affect our heart in a musical way that need not be heard by the outer ear. Most of us have heard the philosophical argument: if a tree falls in a forest and there is no one to hear it, does the falling tree make a sound? I'm not trying to bend our minds but to simply accept other outcomes or be open to different approaches to each and every subject.

In the image of the woman and the saxophone, she has been given much space in front to lead the viewer into the photograph. Take time to gently observe the statement. Here is a person with an instrument holding it carefully, clutching it almost as if she was a novice, not playing, not yet but she is in deep thought, mesmerized by the possibility of playing. It is like the camera is panning towards her and has not yet fully discovered the musician. She isn't fully occupying the space that exists which allows our imagination to fill in what is missing: the rest of her body, her playing the sax, the music and the sound are all left to our imagination, the infinite scenarios. May our photographs reach this stage of wonderment, of art.

As can be seen in the work print on the following page, the lines provide a design to the image and the space or lack of it on the right helps us view the person's face. The composition is not in the usual thirds with the woman moved over and cropped. We can only comprehend part of her story never discovering all there is to know, with so much more unrevealed as it were and always will be.

Let's consider the image size which in itself is of paramount importance. To determine this we must also consider the substrate that we wish to use which in this case was canvas. In addition to using canvas, it was also my suggestion to the client that the overall horizontal length of the image be no smaller than twenty-four or perhaps thirty inches, thereby letting the width define itself. This size enables the viewer to see the image from a reasonable distance, a distance that will allow one to see the image completely and understand the full story. In any art form we need to tell the story or segment of it with impact and completeness in and of itself. Perhaps the image is never done or complete. We can always change things, add, take away, lighten, darken, change colours, never finished, never done and yet because I have printed it, it is expected to be complete. It is now a story to be studied and embellished by the viewers' own distractions, knowledge, creativity and personal experiences.

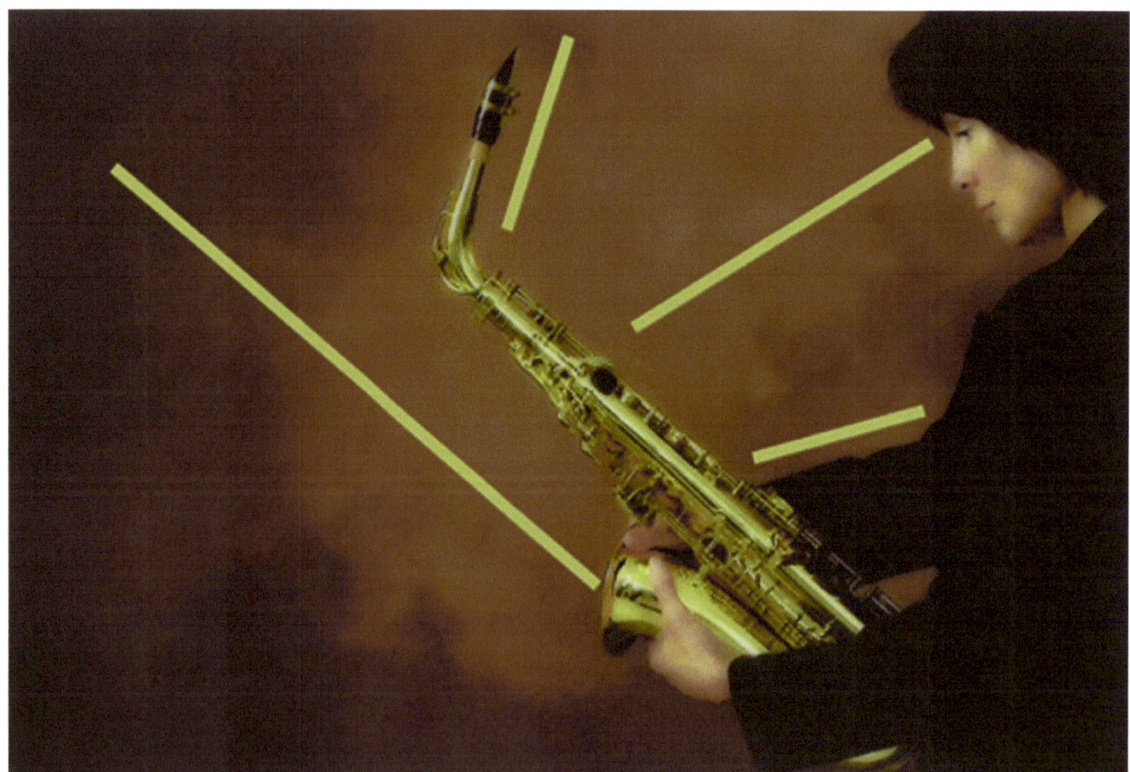

Atypical Executive Portraits

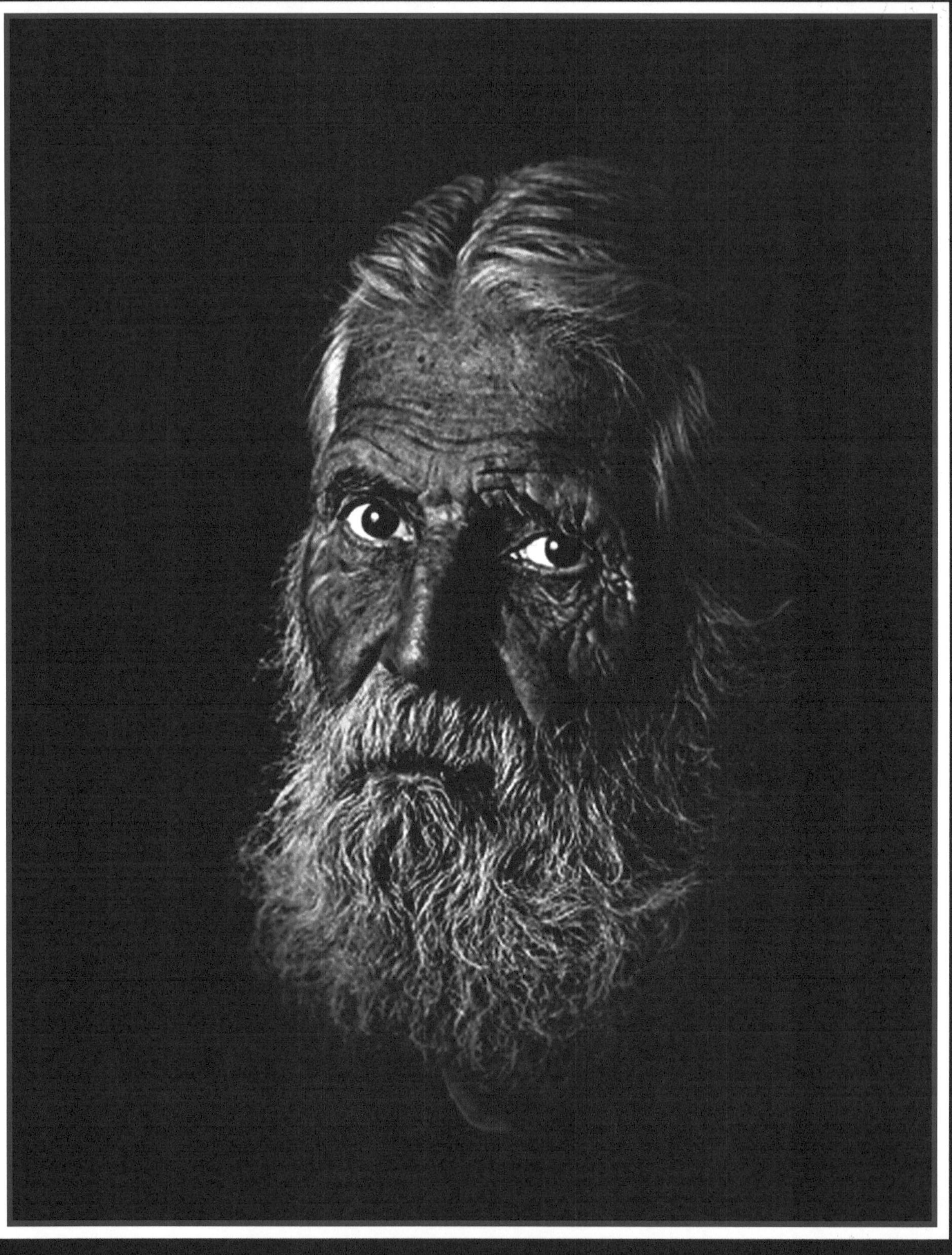

The Prophet

A few years ago when I met this man at one of his seminars he made a profound impression on me. I have read a great deal on natural foods and even raw food diets but reading about it and practicing this healthy lifestyle are quite different. I have done fasts before, a number lasting as long as ten days but more often shorter fasts of three to seven days.

The first time I photographed this man the images showed varying expressions. Two such images are pictured below. These expressions were captured without ever asking for them; they came about naturally through my communication with him on different topics of conversation. I will ***never*** ask someone to smile. It is my professionalism, my voice and body language that provokes a response and it is my intuition that pushes the button on the camera. I never really know when this will happen I just go with the flow of events.

The next year he drove up from California for another seminar which I attended and had an opportunity to photograph him again. This time I wanted to reveal my impression of the man, as unique an individual as I have ever met. He does thousands of fasts with people from all over the world. To me he is like a prophet telling his disciples the truth about healthy living and the philosophy that goes along with living a full and abundant life. The image on the opposite page expresses my interpretation of this man who is determined to get his message out to all who are willing to learn. If you are interested in discovering more about his work you may wish to visit his web site: www.ourplaceinternational.com.

The chiselled face, the piercing eyes, the white beard and the long hair all add to his character and passion for life: natural living. I used a black background to give the illusion that his face is floating, his body is lighter than air, just part of the universe. Looking into his face again and into his eyes, his hair and his beard also tells a story so provocative of this man's lifestyle.

I feel I just couldn't express this more fully than I did in this portrait; a man dedicated to his message, giving of his life to spreading the word.

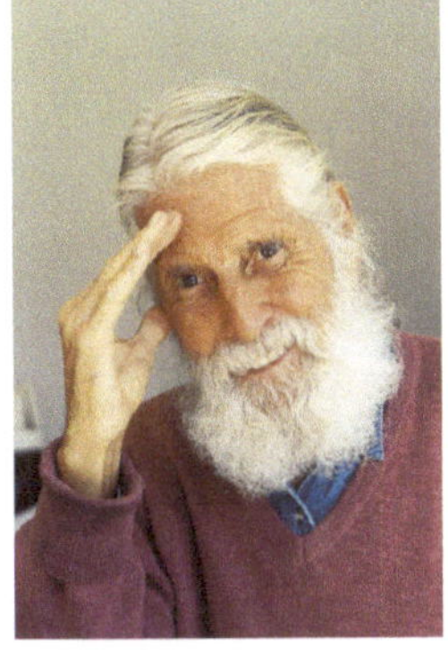

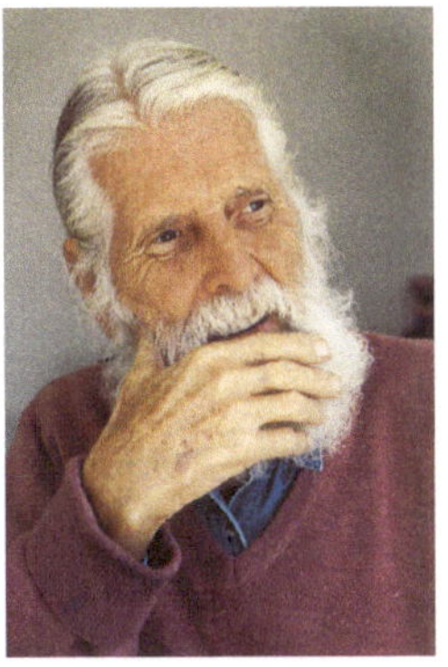

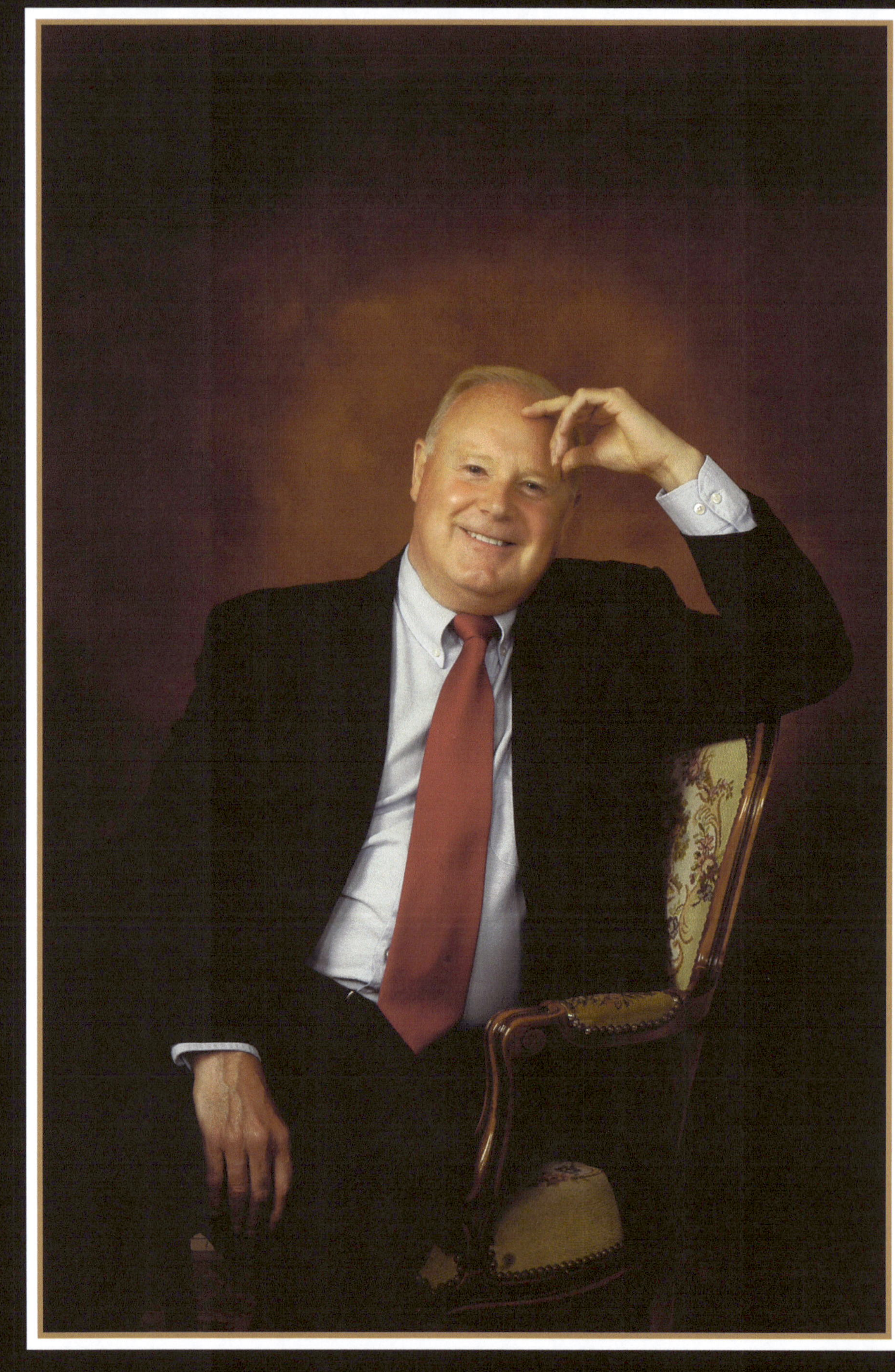

The Inner Man

When this man came into my studio for a portrait to be used for advertising, I asked the usual questions: Where are you from? What do you do? Why do you need an image of yourself?

I discovered that he had just published his first book *Unleashing Your Brilliance*. I looked up his web site as we spoke: www.unleashingbrilliance.com. I found him to be interesting because we had some similar interests like Neuro-Linguistic Programming or NLP, hypnosis, writing and public speaking. As I observed him, he was gentle and refrained from overexerting his knowledge but added to the conversation when it was needed.

This image was my favourite even though he purchased others for his own purposes. Observing the intent and methodical manner of this man I sought to reveal the inner thoughtfulness and wisdom. We can see it in his warm facial expression and the hand up to his forehead suggests much the same. The work print shows his body language with the strength of the box formation and the division of space. There is more space on the left, strong placement in composition with his body leaning to add movement and a quiet action to the overall image. The line at the bottom gives a sense of foundation and stability.

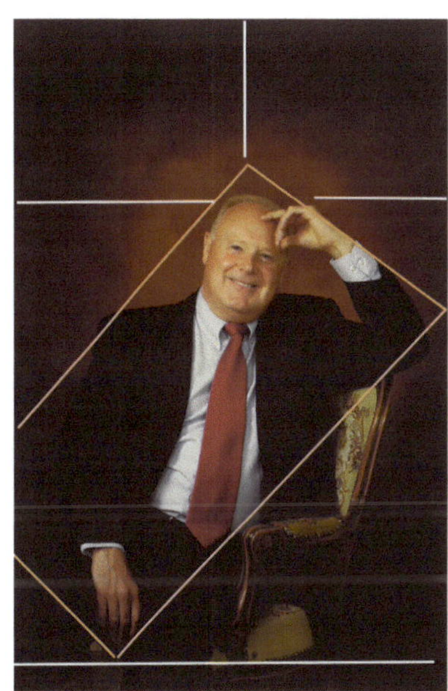

To work within a given space as is the confinement in still photography the elements of design are crucial. As can be seen, the pulling apart of certain elements in the image with lines gives the viewer a chance to comprehend the basis of the photo. It may be less evident to grasp these nuances without mapping out these elements.

We can see the picture but can we read the elements or the photographic language that may be hidden to even the most aspiring photographer?

An artist once told me, "Klaus, if you put tracing paper over the photograph as you explained it to me, the lines on the tracing paper would be pleasing to the eye." Of course everything in nature can be reduced to lines in a most basic way.

May we want to learn the eloquent expression of photography which is truly a universal language akin to painting and music even though so often we may think of photography as a stepchild to painting.

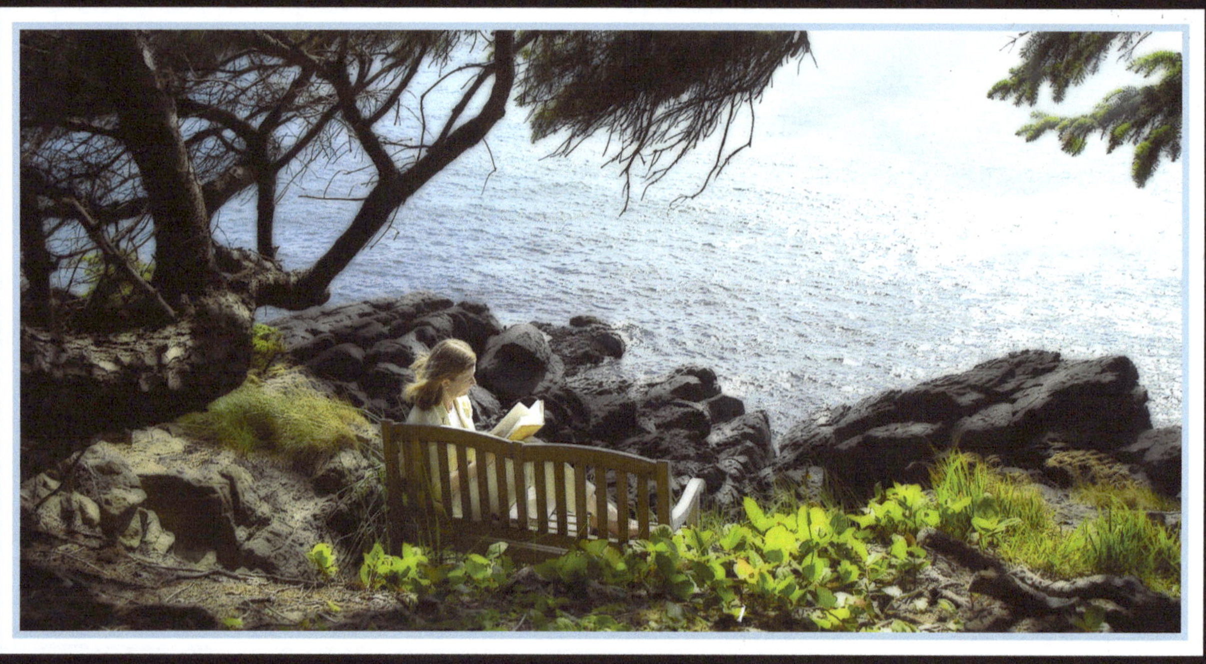

Beauty in Nature

I was commissioned to photograph this woman as a birthday present from her husband at their beautiful waterfront home on the west coast of Vancouver Island. As with most people she was concerned about her expressions and how she would look with the wind blowing. I explained that we usually see ourselves in a mirror which is the reverse of our true self that others see. I promised that her image would be enhanced so as to be more truthful or perfect to satisfy her mind's eye.

Upon our arrival we were given the grand tour and picked a few spots in the home and also explored the outdoors which represented endless possibilities. The husband and wife were photographed together and then I concentrated on her alone to produce an art piece that would compliment the rest of the art on their walls. I felt that a romantic type of photograph on watercolour paper would be a possibility. Since reading is one of her passions a book was chosen and we went to her favourite spot. The wind blew a little which was in harmony with the setting, her experiences in this special place and was just how she had described it to me.

Sitting there reading, hearing the wind and feeling the breeze on her face is something she loves and this impression is reinforced and layered by an indelible, unforgettable and permanent experience in her thoughts. Take a close look at the breathtaking sky and the trees framing the story overall; the softness of the image, the location of the subject on the bench at the bottom part of the photograph, the rocks and yet in all there is a serenity, a peacefulness in spite of what we may imagine it to be like.

I have often said that my photographs are like my babies because there is always a story in the background unbeknownst to the photograph's viewer: the story of how they met, when they found this acreage and its one of a kind placement by the ocean. Words would fail me if I tried to explain all this in mere prose.

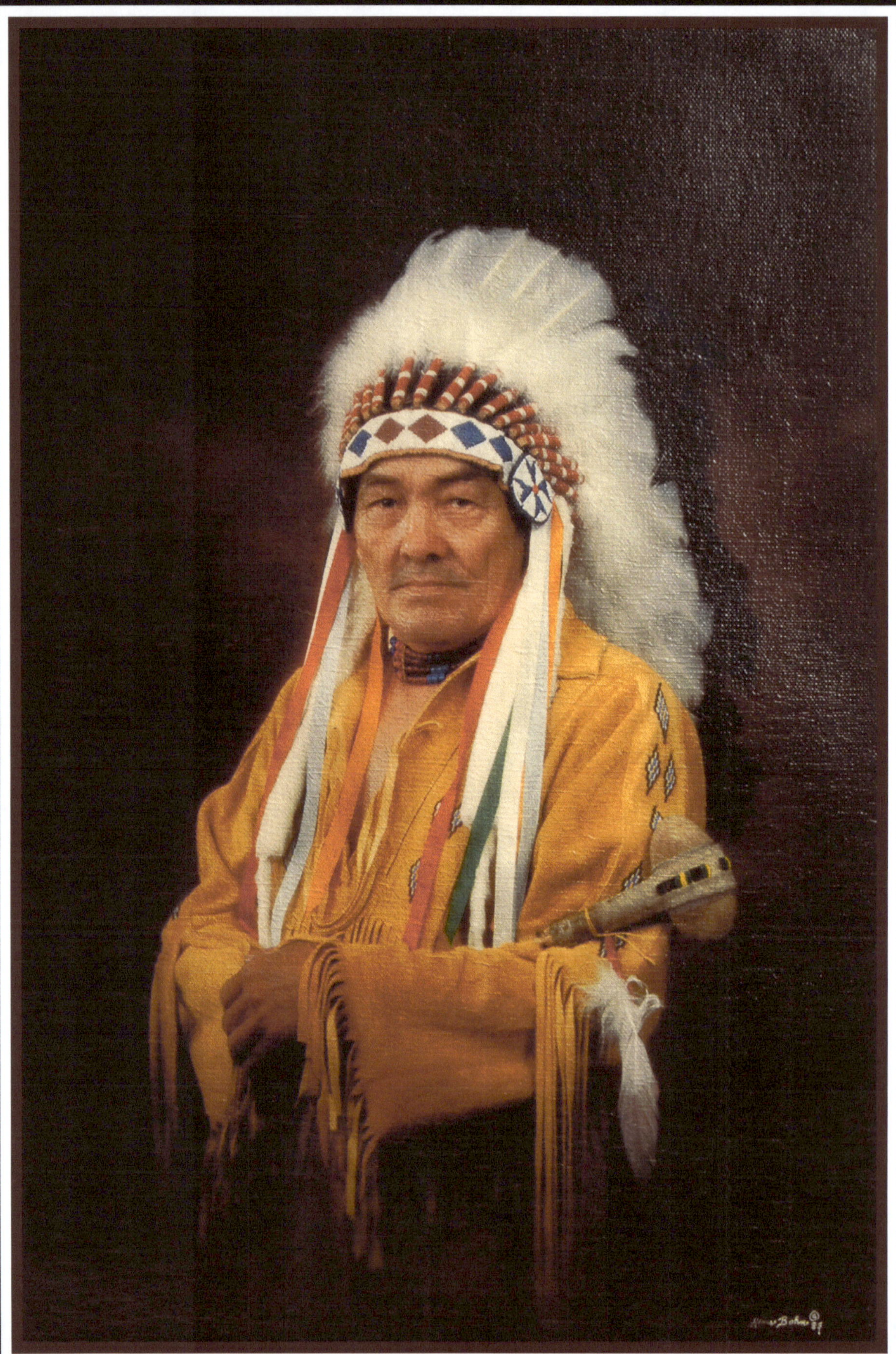

A Chiefly Honour

This photograph was taken when my studio was in Moose Jaw, Saskatchewan, and at that time there were only a few natives living in the town. This man's daughter was living in Regina and one day while visiting her father she walked in and inquired if I would be interested in taking a traditional, old style image of her father with head dress and clothing so as to represent his heritage. I jumped at the opportunity to photograph a man with so much dignity and honour. He was more than willing to participate; not only for his daughter but to have a record of his past and to create a connection with the present generations to keep memories of their culture from fading.

I enjoyed photographing this man because not only was he very enthusiastic but he was also very funny and I felt we made a real connection. He told me of the scar on his side and jokingly said, "I was wounded by a spear in battle.'' In reality I believe he was wounded in World War II. I am not completely certain but whatever it was it made for a good story anyway. Stories are passed down in native culture from generation to generation so the essence remains but at the same time the story can grow with embellishments and flowery anecdotes that may not have been present in the original story. As I listened to him I could see this storytelling happening over generations – the same story over and over again growing and become more entertaining with each retelling.

Looking at the photograph I believe we can see into this man's history. His eyes are sad as he holds the tomahawk protectively and he set his face like flint, the leathered look enhanced by the canvas' texture. The oval composition is completed by the headdress. It is sad that the past is sometimes left behind or forgotten, mourned in darkness and only retold by a few.

He is turned slightly as if to say, "You cannot face my past but I need to come to the future, the present, and yet I'm so unwilling because of the pain of the past." He wears the headdress as a symbol of pride and authority, the buckskin jacket covering his physical wounds and his face as a mask covering the emotional scars of his people's history.

Words beg for definition, for understanding. *Feeling* this image still jars me when I take the time to really look and see. It is not a Hollywood image, a glamour shot or a pretty picture. Maybe a poem, a song that could be sung around the camp fire or perhaps it is a story that cannot be told or remembered because it is too far in the past and the only thing that remains is the feeling of being a misfit in one's own time and country.

*"Photography is a sad art;
it is only alive for a fraction of a second,
and they never get older in the picture."
-Richard Avedon*

*"Photographers deal in things which are
continually vanishing and when they have
vanished there is no contrivance on earth
which can make them come back again."
-Henri Cartier-Bresson*

Our Cherished Families

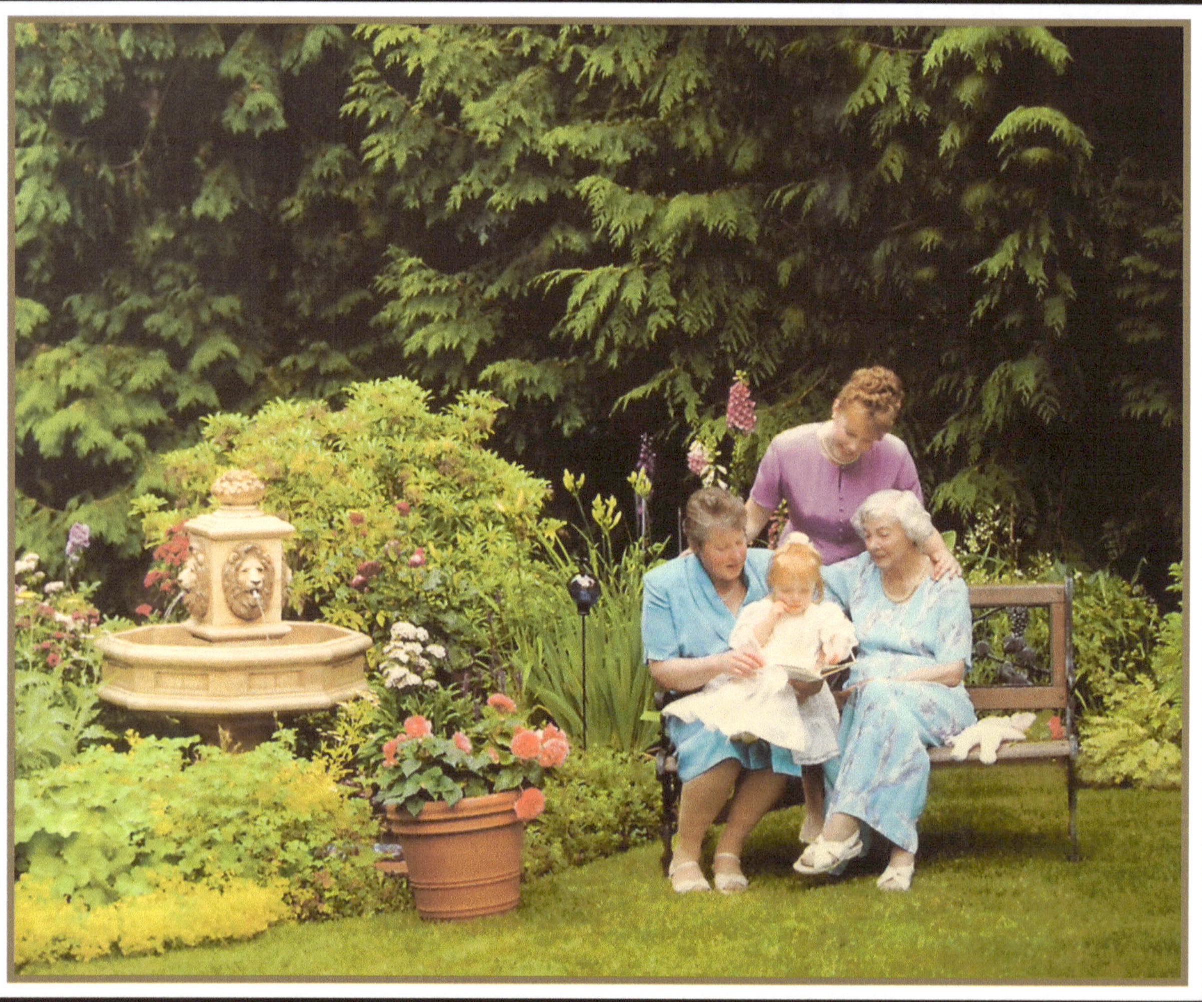

Four Generations

When the parents of the little girl came for their consultation a number of decisions were made straight away. First of all it was going to be a photograph capturing four generations and it would be taken in their backyard. To create a focal point within the photograph it was decided that they would be reading a book to the little girl. The most difficult decision was the finish. We had over seven finishes to choose from and the final choice was to have the image printed on watercolour paper for longevity. This enabled the background and grass to be enhanced plus a layer of digital effect to add more texture.

The background needed some additional work because there were large gaps in the trees and they needed to be filled in with branches. There was grass missing under and behind the bench, so the cosmetics were taken care of by adding a toned down cross hatch effect. We decided not to go too far in making this image look to painterly but just enough for the viewer to appreciate that something was done to the image.

The left to right composition as shown in the work print on the next page leads the eye quickly and almost without notice to the three women involved with the child and book, its very purpose. The faces needed to have more of a watercolour look so to speak and there was the added challenge of having all four subjects look at the book with natural expressions to tie it all together. I had to provide a lot of verbal cues because inevitably there was always one person who wanted to look directly at me or the camera. We addressed this during the consultation.

From my experience I know that to achieve a photograph like this it needed to be taken at the end of the photographic session. I began with everyone looking at me, at the camera, and we were successful in capturing some fun photographs. Then the next stage was to have everyone looking at each other with big smiles. In order to tone down their smiles I spoke softly and when we brought the book out the stage was set! I like to work quickly when the end result is in sight and the hands and expressions are co-ordinated. The little girl's mother has her arms around all three with both the grandmother's and great-grandmother's hands displaying just the right degree of participation. The great-grandmother's legs were crossed to focus the viewer's eyes back into the image before leaving the photograph. One may also notice the doll on the bench as part of the layout but it plays a minor role.

I like the circular movement over the objects in the yard which lead us to the people and hold us there because of the primary interest, the storytelling activity. The heads form an elliptical shape and also somewhat of a diamond shape. Remember everything is made out of shapes and without shapes there would be nothing, at least nothing distinguishable.

The feeling in this image is expressed in the face of each subject. The child is pensive and taken up with what is in the book, her little hand is reaching up to her face in wonderment. Her mother is happy and enjoying this awe inspiring moment, a privileged moment to have all four generations together at her home and to preserve a moment in time for generations to come. So often we don't put forth the effort to preserve memories because it takes effort and sometimes money. The grandmother is perhaps even more involved because she is reading out loud for all to enjoy, especially her granddaughter. Last but by no means least the great-grandmother, the one who began this cycle of life is participating gently and quietly. I wonder what was going on in her mind, thoughts of the past when she was little or looking towards the future when other family members will look back at this photograph and wonder too.

The leading line from the far left brings the viewer into the image on a gentle line as it were, under tension slightly with an up and down motion. The photo's strength is portrayed as the subjects are in the right hand thirds and are positioned in a circular motion to keep the eye captivated within that part of the photograph just a little longer. Study the expressions, the storytelling, the book. The depth and movement are easy to enjoy and be comforted in a pleasant, peaceful setting that brings such joy.

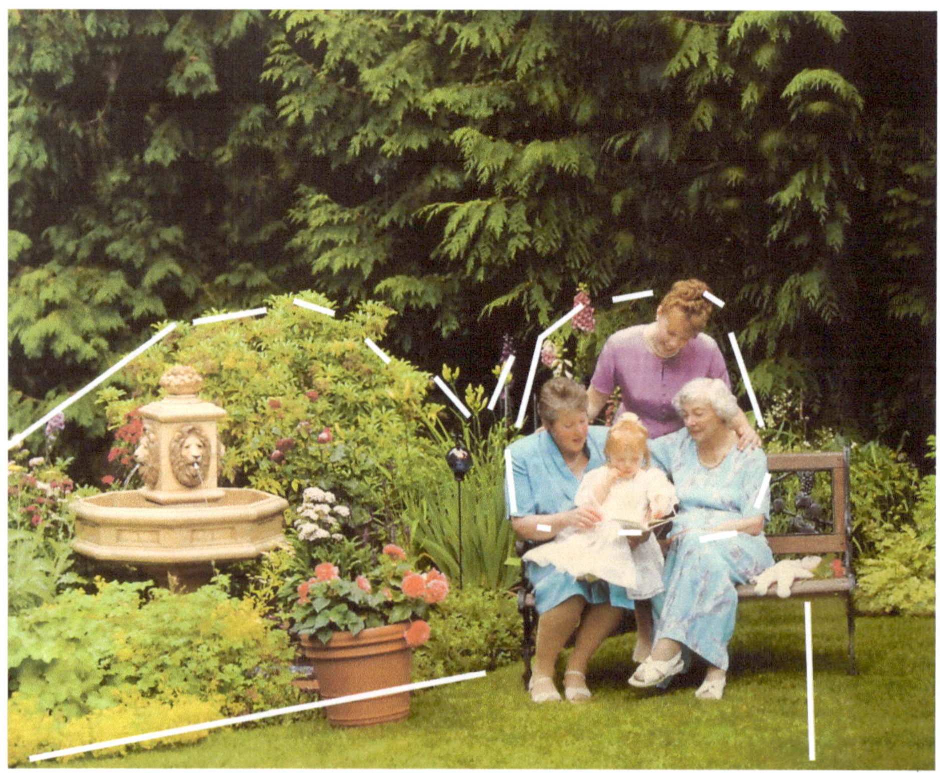

"Our truth lies in what we love."
-Klaus Bohn

"I never question what to do, it tells me what to do.
The photographs make themselves with my help."
-Ruth Bernhard

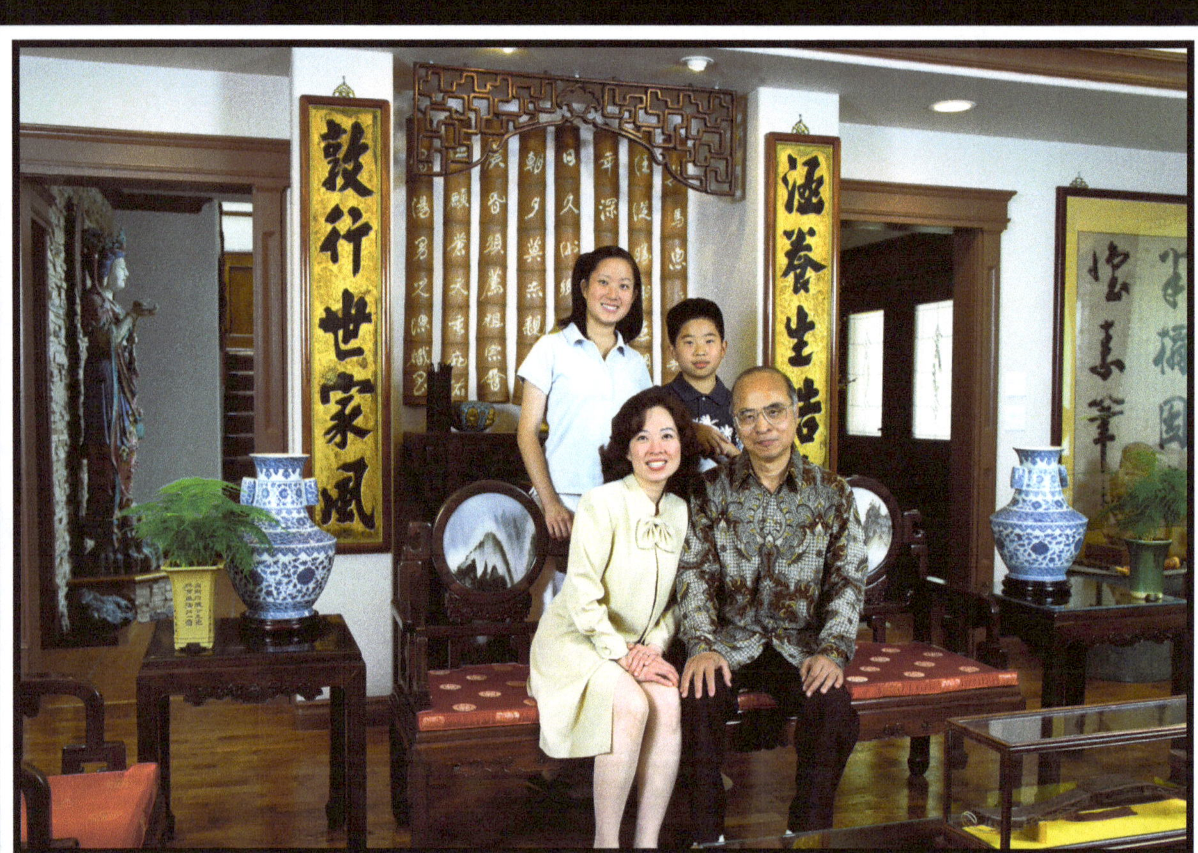
敦行世家風
涵養生吉

A Close Family

The husband and wife made an appointment to have a consultation and family photographs taken in their home. The outside of their house wasn't overbearing or ostentatious but inside the art pieces, vases, statues and wall hangings impressed me to the point that I knew they would appreciate my work if I included some treasured pieces in the photographs as well as more of a statuesque portrait of the family.

I arrived with my two sons Michael and David with equipment to spare. "Be careful," I told my sons, "there are many precious artifacts in every room of the house." All three of us were in awe as the wife took some time to show us around explaining the value of what was in a very large glass case that was filled with very small women's shoes. In the past Asian women restricted the growth of their feet, which was a sign of beauty.

The arrangement of the subjects was very formal as I felt their spirit, body language and home dictated this to me. The father sat very erect and his wife nestled close beside him. Of course the son needed to be close to the father and the daughter near her mother but in behind them to show proper placement and respect within their culture.

The cropping may be somewhat unusual but I cropped the wife's feet for obvious cultural reasons. The door on the left was kept open for the eye to travel past the statue and up the stairs while the open door on the right also allowed light in. The main difficulty encountered was to illuminate the wall hanging behind them without flaring light and keeping the colour true, all the while concentrating on the family and their expressions. We need to understand that overtly large smiles were predicated by our beloved Hollywood and not from the old world or even in other societies. A more natural smile or expression somehow makes the subjects in any work seem more human, more real.

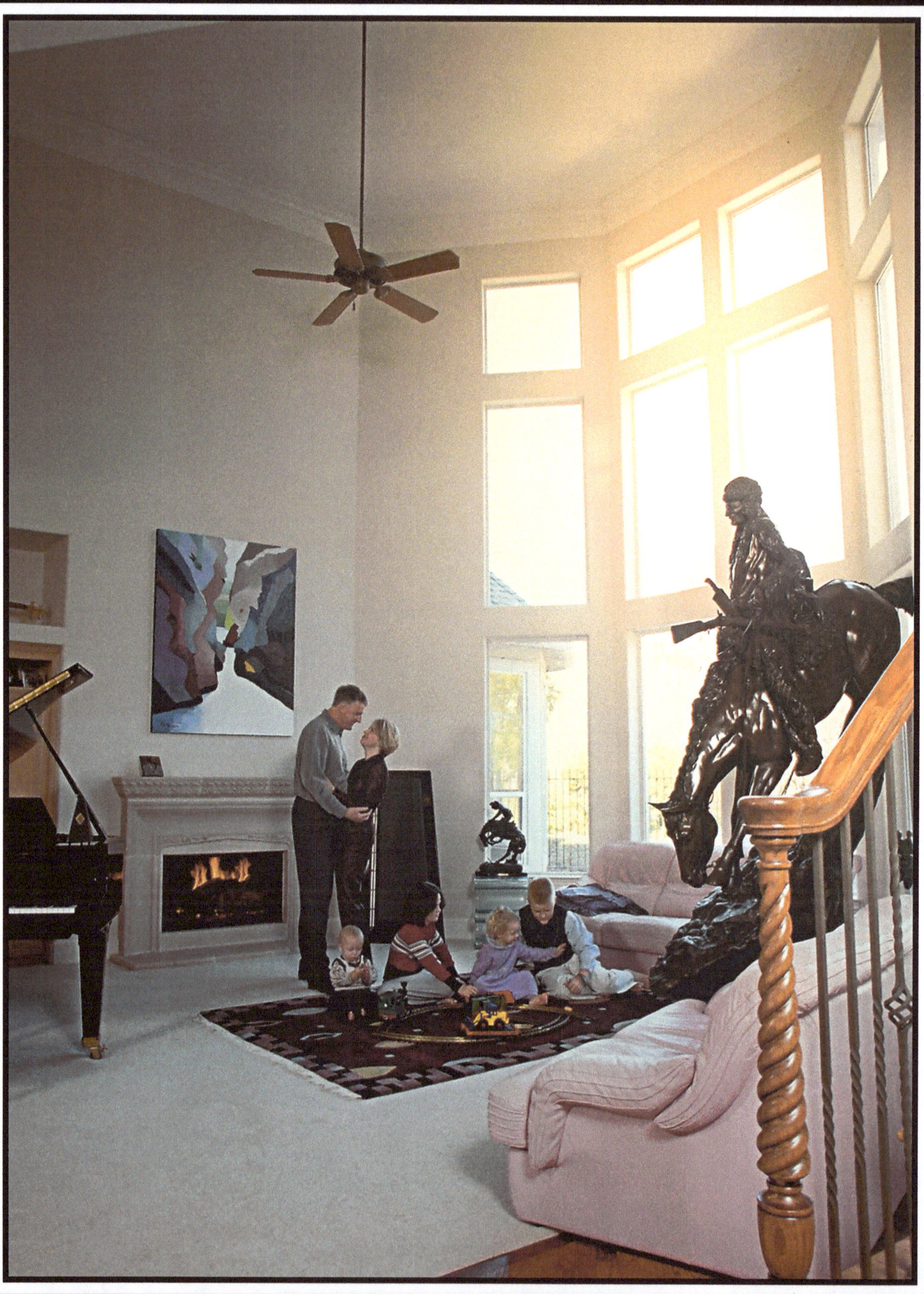

Everything's Bigger in Texas

The parents in the photograph were looking at my work and were especially taken with the image of a family sitting around a pool. This very successful heart surgeon told me that they where building a negative edge or infinity pool and wondered if I would be willing to go to Dallas, Texas, to photograph his family. I immediately agreed but in the back of my mind I was thinking that this may not take place because of our schedules. Over the years I have photographed many weddings in the United States and different parts of Canada. As you can imagine it takes a lot of work to co-ordinate everything but it almost always turns out to be a rewarding and enriching experience for both myself and my clients. The phone call came in November, a very busy time for photographers. However being true to my word and always fulfilling my commitments I flew down to Dallas and had the privilege to stay with this family in their home.

In addition to the photographic session, this trip was filled with new and exciting experiences. Upon my arrival I was picked up and given an outline of what we would be doing over the next three days and was taken out for dinner at a very nice restaurant. The next day I met some of the husband's colleagues and later that evening we went to a basketball game featuring NBA All-Star Steve Nash. By spending so much time with the entire family I was able to learn how best to photograph them in their environment. Their youngest son took a special liking to me and I enjoyed our time together too.

Having had a chance to discuss and evaluate the different possible locations to photograph the family, I felt pressure because it turned out that I needed to pick up some lighting equipment that I didn't bring with me. The husband generously offered to purchase whatever I needed. However, hoping to simply rent the necessary equipment, we went into a camera store with a lot of second hand inventory. At first the man behind the counter told us that he could not rent us the equipment but then the owner, who had overheard our conversation asked, "Where are you from?" I told him that I was visiting from Victoria, British Columbia, Canada. He said, "I have been there and like the city very much, why don't you rent my equipment?" So we ended up doing just that.

The big shoot was on the next day and I wanted to photograph the family before everyone got too tired, dirty and so on. The main challenge I had was with light. The sunlight outside was so bright that I needed a bank of lights on the left side by the piano to balance the natural light as well as to pick up the fireplace. I am providing you with details of some of the difficulties I encountered so that as one studies the image the end result may be seen in a better light. Please excuse the pun. Their young son had become so friendly with me that he kept crawling to me instead of staying where I placed him. The focus needed to be taken away from me and the equipment and have him play with the toys near his siblings, while keeping the parents where I wanted them, looking at each other. I wanted it this way because it is a blended family. It was important to show the relationship the children have with each other and the bonding of two people in a unique but understandable way.

Let us take a look at the U-shape in the image which I wasn't even conscious of until an artist illustrated this very point: the lines on the work print from the fan down through the couple and back up through the large statue. Also please note the depth from the staircase to the bay window and trees that can be seen through the windows. The echo of the little statue on the far side of the room helps to reveal the scale of the larger statue and the size of the man on the horse's back is amplified in this way as well. The subtle presence of the piano on the left adds shape and design for the viewer to enter into the image. I wanted the space overhead because I like the way Thomas Gainsborough, one of the most famous portrait and landscape painters of eighteenth century Britain, painted with so much space above his clients. To truly appreciate the vastness of the space being portrayed, the image needs to be a large size such as the 40-inch print they purchased.

The storytelling within this image has a long lasting effect, even on me. As I often mention during my consultations, each image I display on my walls are like my children. They have a history, are part of me, and I find this to be true for almost every photograph I take.

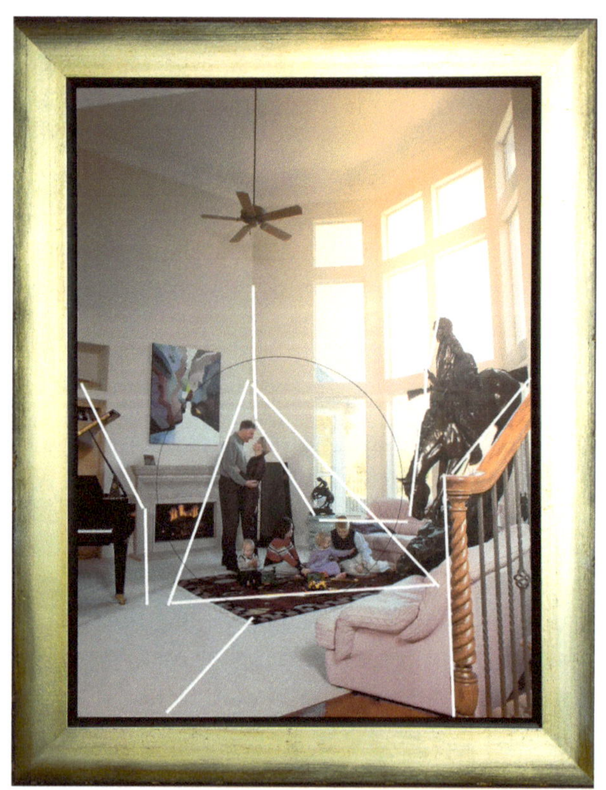

"My portraits are more about me
than they are about the people I photograph."
-Richard Avedon

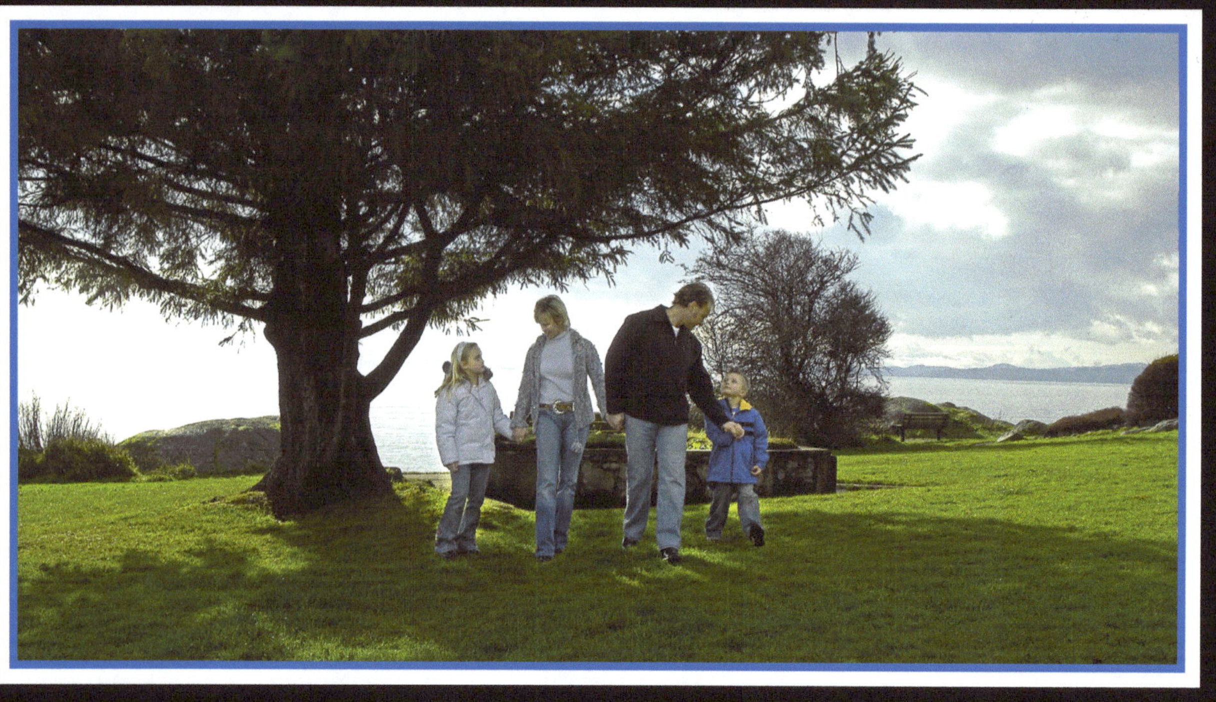

A Family in Harmony

There are so many beautiful places on Vancouver Island where the ocean is part of the background and naturally enhances any scene. During my consultation with this family their choice was to be near the ocean because they live in that area and go for walks along the ocean. What a perfect place to be photographed. It was late November I believe, so the air was cool. Their clothing and interactions were in total harmony with the way they surely have walked together along this familiar stretch of shore.

I wanted to capture the feeling of a family naturally doing what they normally do when the photographer is not present. My brief instructions were, "Just walk towards me and look and talk to one another." My son David was operating the camera as I talked to the family to capture an excitement and a flow as they walked together hand in hand as parents naturally do with a young family.

The flow of the composition brings us into the photograph with a natural rhythm and movement. There may be shortcomings in an art piece with depth only being implied. However when we look at this image our eyes flow from left to right and pick up the rhythm of the family as they walk, adding another suggestion of reality and movement. The depth can be appreciated when we see past the family towards the left where there is space for the eye to travel out upon the water to a far away place, perhaps changing our perception through our mind's experiences. Balance has been harmonized with the expanse of the image being narrow and horizontally long like movies in a theatre.

At the beginning of my career my Dad once asked me, "Why do you take so many photographs with an up and down orientation? Why not sideways?" as he put it. I must confess that back then I really didn't understand his point because magazines at that time printed almost every photograph vertically. Then I visited Europe and a photographer asked me the same question, "Why do North American photographers choose the vertical composition so often?" Finally it clicked when he said, "Since our eyes are side by side we tend to see at least twenty percent more when an image has a horizontal versus vertical orientation." Then I understood that we have a choice. Let us make choices in photography as in life and not just copy what others have done before us.

Our natural means of communication seems to be verbal but that isn't always so. In still photography we communicate through body language, a mere suggestion to be read by those who have learned the language, the art of photography, to read the image.

Studying the image, absorb that which can be learned and then refined and expanded so you can take photography to the next level through your own experiences.

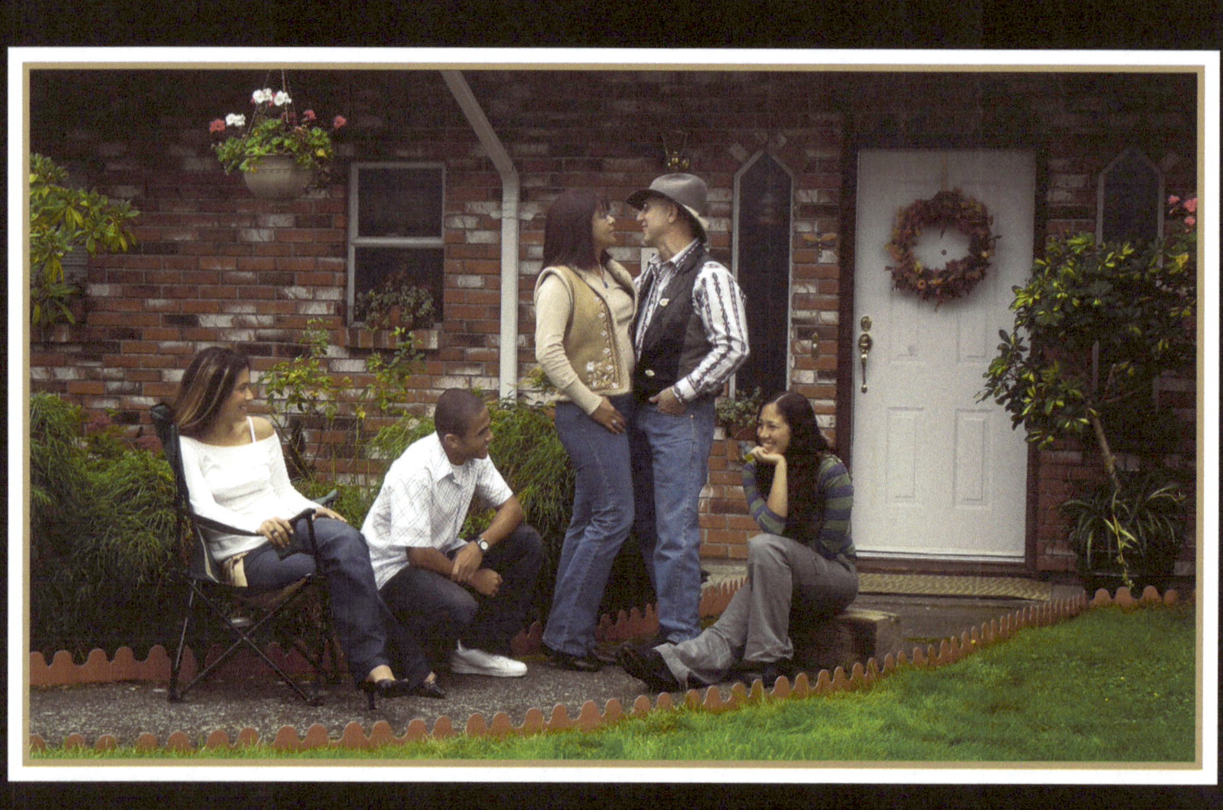

Faces Never Lie

The mother and one of her daughters came in for a consultation to set up a photographic session at their house. They were very friendly and told me how they moved to Victoria, British Columbia, from Mexico several years ago. She had met her new husband when he was working in Mexico and eventually immigrated to Canada with her children. The idea was to create a fun family photo, showing their special relationship while combining the kids within this format.

We shared ideas and concerns we might have and I did my best to answer their questions. I took the time to visit their home and discussed where the photograph may hang in their house and found a perfect place. Now we knew the size and shape the image needed to be. The mother's concern wasn't that the faces should be totally visible but rather that the heartfelt happiness would show on everyone's faces. It is not easy to accomplish this. However I believe this family portrait accomplishes this request quite well. At least that is what they told me when they picked up the photograph. The decision to photograph the family outdoors was made during my visit and we all agreed that it should be in the front along the path, the path that will always lead their family back home.

When examining the image, the design, the flow, the joy and the happiness, the feeling of a close family is echoed in their expressions. It is all about the feeling of a family, blended or otherwise, together with love for one another through thick and thin, truly unmasking the face we so often hide behind but cannot fake because our soul comes through. I love families and that is one reason I am a family photographer. I have spent most of my career photographing families. I love my family no matter what. Even though my own children are grown they will always be my children; always in my heart, always in my thoughts, thinking about them every day. Their pain becomes my pain, their joy my joy and I'm glad that I can live with it either way, in all ways and for all my life.

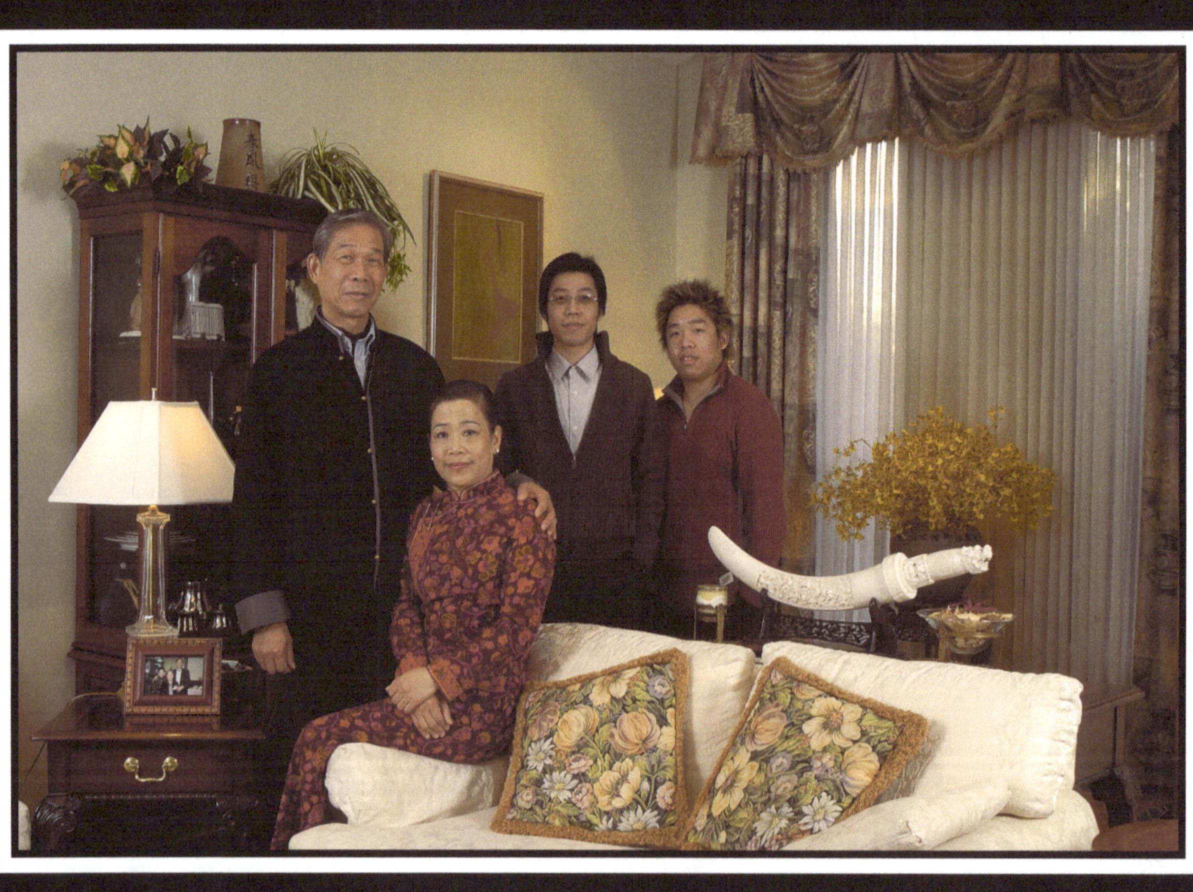

Respect for Family Traditions

When I was invited to photograph this family in their home I needed to understand a little more about their culture, beliefs and traditions. We had a consultation in their home which made it easier to plan the end result: where it will hang, what size would be appropriate for the space, what would be the best composition, head size, how much space around them, etc.

As one studies the work print on the next page keep in mind the subjects' traditions, background and culture because it is my duty as a professional photographer to respect them. The design works with space and the depth of the image is sensed by the positioning of one object in front of the other such as the placement of the father above yet close to the mother with the older son in behind followed by his younger brother next to but also slightly behind him.

The sword carving behind the sofa was interesting and important to them so we gave it the honour it deserved in their home. The lamp on the left helps balance the sword carving on the right, asymmetrical beauty and composition, along with the colour of the sofa which also worked well into the overall composition. Normally I do not move items on walls or furniture too much when photographing in a home environment. This is especially true when working with a client for the first time. Additionally, if I move things too much, they might believe that I think their home is out of order and it can be perceived as an insult. It is always better to tread lightly and compromise one's own values and design beliefs. For example, the plant on top of the glass cabinet could have been moved but I made a judgement call to leave it in its place. We opened the curtain slightly to allow a little more light to come through for a greater feeling of depth. The subjects are in harmony with complimentary expressions.

When working in a home environment I need to be in control. Control with a gentle touch and respect is the key. I always show respect for my client so they will show respect for me, the artist, in return. In this way we can feel comfortable with one another, even if we don't fully understand each other's language. Our respect is felt and then can be reciprocated. This mutual respect and understanding allows me to voice my opinions during the projection, thereby permitting them to have a better appreciation for my design concepts.

This thirty-six inch wide wall portrait had a perfect impact at the size I suggested because the photograph was going in a larger room, which provided the appropriate viewing distance. The small framed photograph under the lamp is like a postage stamp mimicking the much more significant larger image.

Photographers are so fortunate to be able to share their interest and knowledge of photography, sharing and giving to others even if only in a modest way.

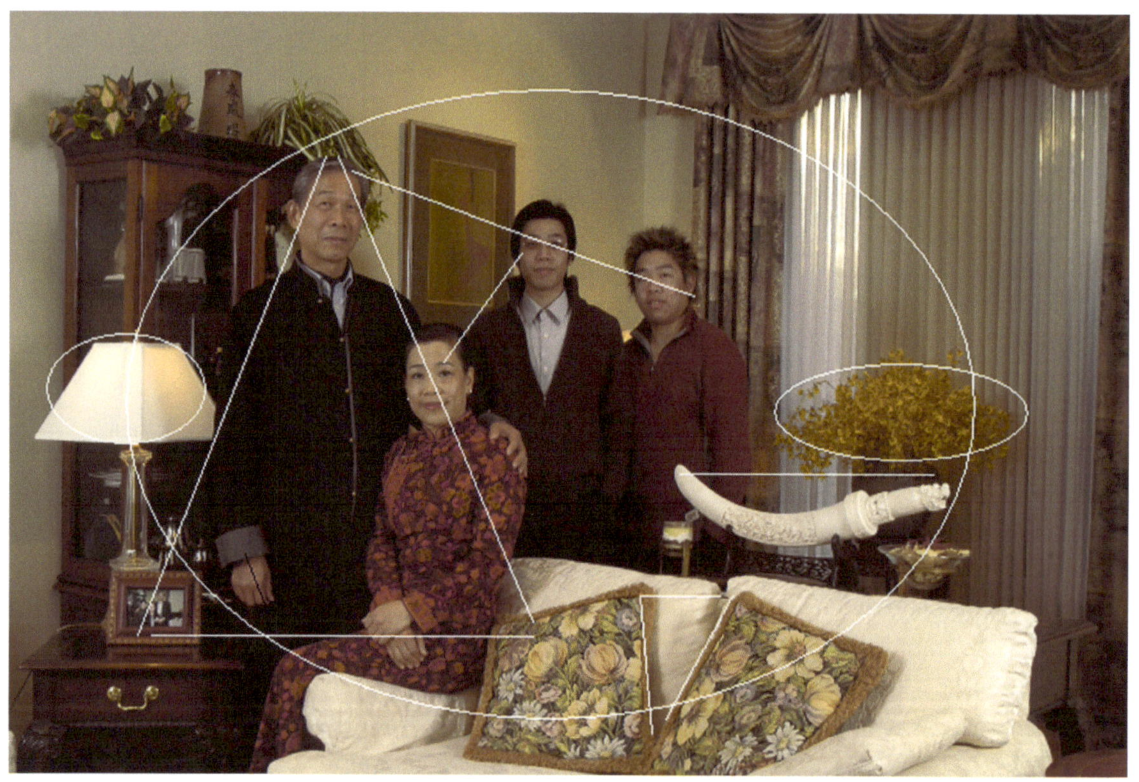

"There are always two people in every picture:
the photographer and the viewer."
-Ansel Adams

"Creativity has no time line;
it is faster than the blink of an eye
but slower than a lifetime."
-Klaus Bohn

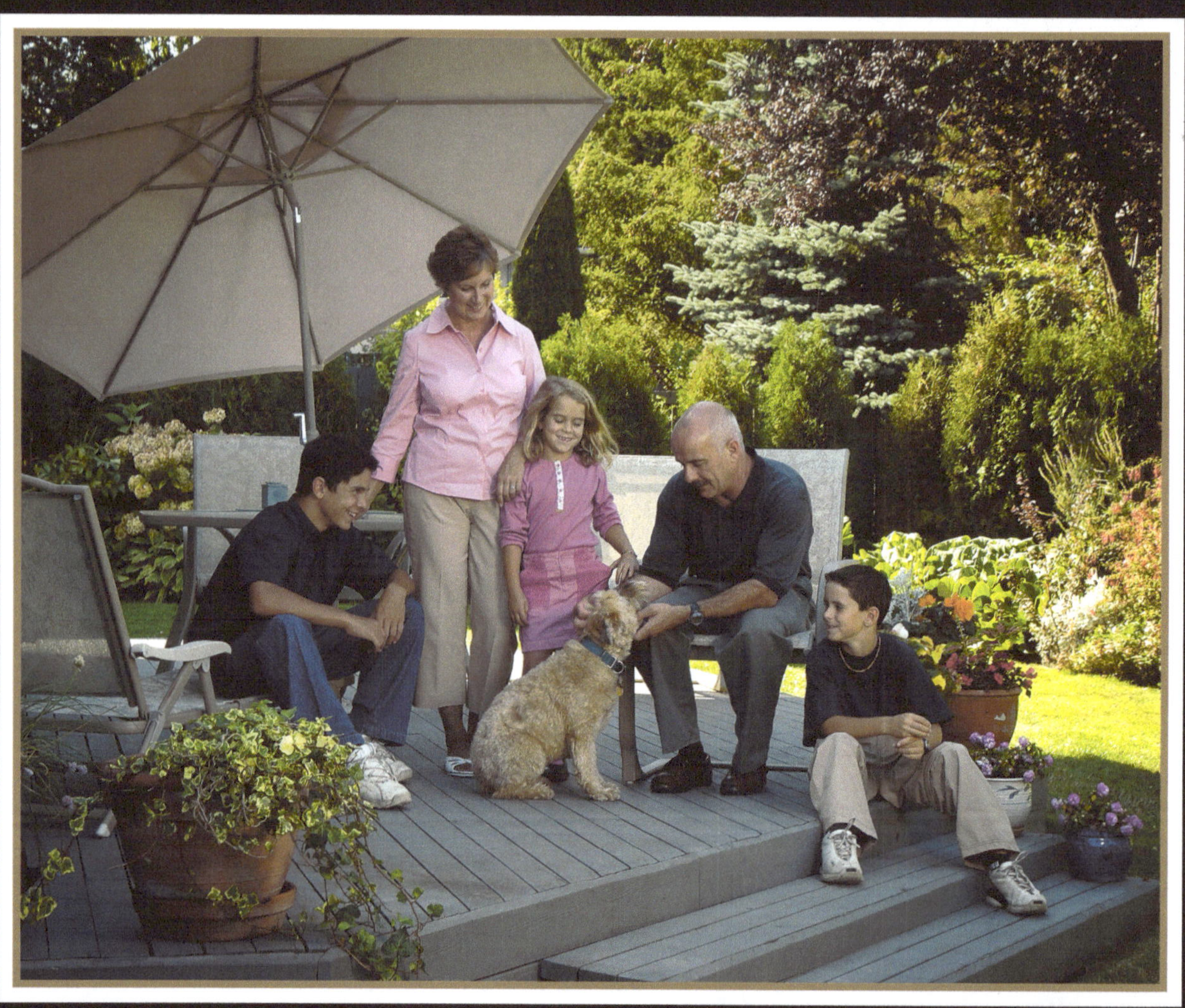

Unconditional Love

During the consultation the mother mentioned to me that one of her sons never smiles because he is self conscious about his teeth. I said to her that it would be okay as not very many of my photographs emphasize smiles. Keeping the expressions natural for the image allows the composition to reveal the truth about a moment in time. The key is not thinking about the camera but allowing the photographer to extract the expressions in harmony with one another. It is not always an easy task to accomplish as anyone who has tried to produce a portrait knows only too well.

When we gathered together the natural lighting was very bright so we chose a place in the backyard on the deck to keep the brightness down to a minimum. I often use a bare bulb or a soft box to enhance the lighting and it was possible to create this set up in spite of the bright day overall. I like to work at my convenience and not necessarily when the weather is the best or the light is perfect. I'm very selfish with my time. My two sons were working with me and they set up the equipment while I concentrated on the subjects and was able to see their reactions as we communicated.

Even when I don't work alone, envisioning the design and setting up the composition is my privilege, my responsibility, my way of seeing. Looking at this photograph, many of the compositional principles or elements discussed in my first book are evident: pyramids, leading lines, movement, depth through use of foreground and background, interaction with subjects and focal point. All these and many more are taking place, all the while capturing natural expressions with the subjects having no sense of my directorial influence.

Study the photograph to see some of the lines suggested throughout the image to knit the family together in harmony. Notice the overlapping of bodies and the connection of body and chair to complete the scene. Take particular note of the expression on their faces, a feeling of unity, and the center of interest is their beloved pet. Dogs are a part of many families. We all serve and love in an unselfish way because dogs can do so little for us except make us happy when we play with them, feed them and take them for walks even if we don't feel like it. They help us become less selfish and more giving, even if we don't want to. That is what a family is; to give to each other that which we might never give to one another, unconditional love and understanding.

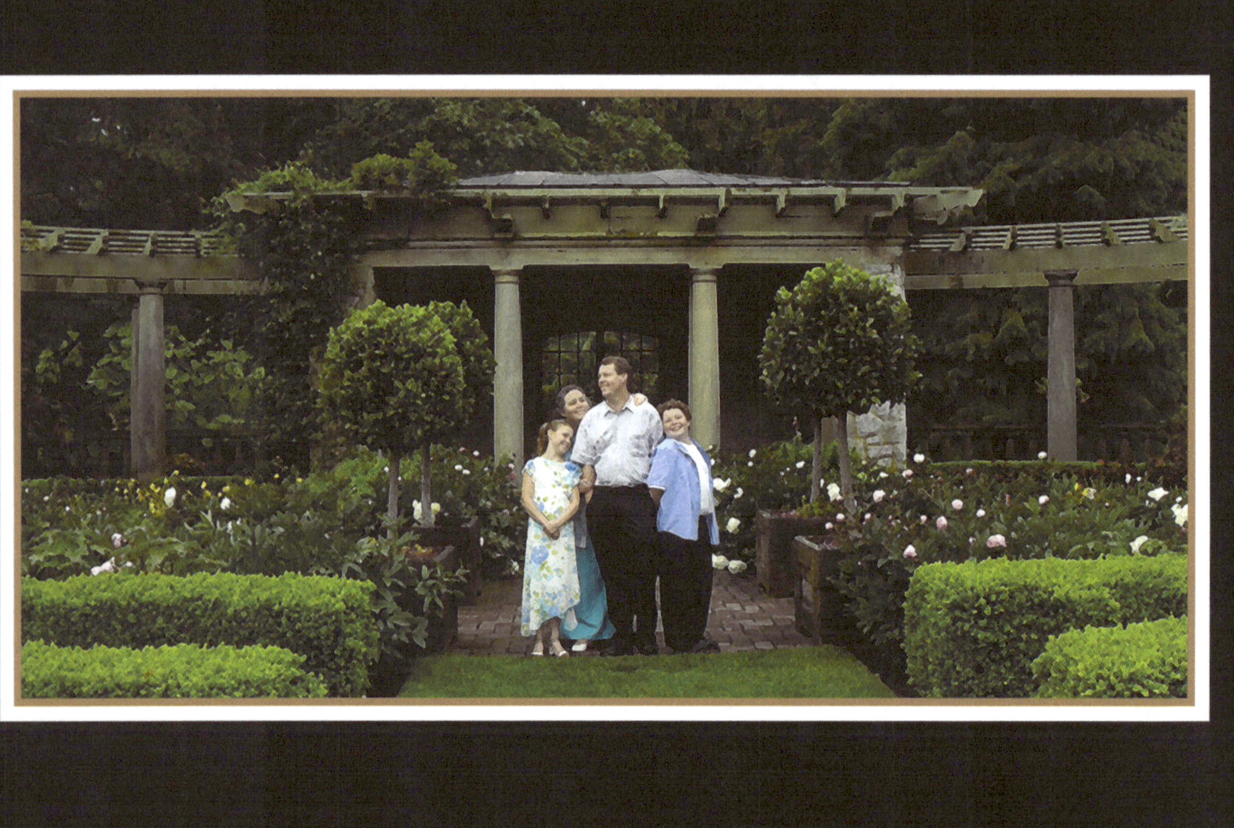

A Family in Unison

Having met the father many years before in Saskatchewan, he was already familiar with my style of photography. His wife though had more traditional ideas and didn't want photos taken without at least some of their faces showing. My suggestion was to photograph her family in the manner she requested while capturing a few more images that may express who they are to me. She agreed.

The children and parents really enjoyed the experience. This may be partly due to the fact that I never force an expression or initially pose them in a difficult way. The image that the mother thought she would never purchase drew her interest as an additional piece for their living room. It is not pictured here but yes, it happened to be a photo shot from the back. I like to surprise my clients in wonderful ways because we live in a land and time of rapid changes, a surprise around every corner. How could we ever get bored? If we do, it is because our minds are not yet fully developed to see beyond what has been real and what will be real for us just micro seconds away. Are we ready for what we are expecting? Is the best yet to come without searching or forcing the issue, just letting it happen, walking through open doors?

The members of this family are woven around the father, the husband. I loved the relationship I could see even at the beginning of the session, a respected husband and father with kindness generated from his being, which I could appreciate so much.

The location is a favourite with film makers, so many Hollywood movies having had a glimpse of this place. Yes, the campus of Royal Roads University in Victoria, British Columbia gets crowded and there are people forever walking into the scene, so patience is a necessity. All this adds to the excitement and memory making experience for all, especially the kids. Memory making is what every good parent wants to leave with the ones we love the most, our children.

There is a panoramic feel that envelops the family as they are wrapped together in the middle of the image almost bending the outer edge back around as it were. At least that is what the father said when he saw the image for the first time. He is an amateur photographer with a good eye and appreciated the effort and talent that went into making all the photographs that were captured that day.

Looking at the image we can see how the placement of the family breaks the conventional rules of thirds, is dead center, framed within the two main pillars, etc., and yet gives us a feeling as if it might have happened naturally without any direction. My desire is that even though we know portraits are not accidents, the viewer should feel that an uncanny experience took place. Study the lines and impact as it shapes this image in a way that is unique unto itself. I have never composed an image like this before. Be open to every new possibility and adventure that comes your way and make the outcome real in itself. It is all about making memories!

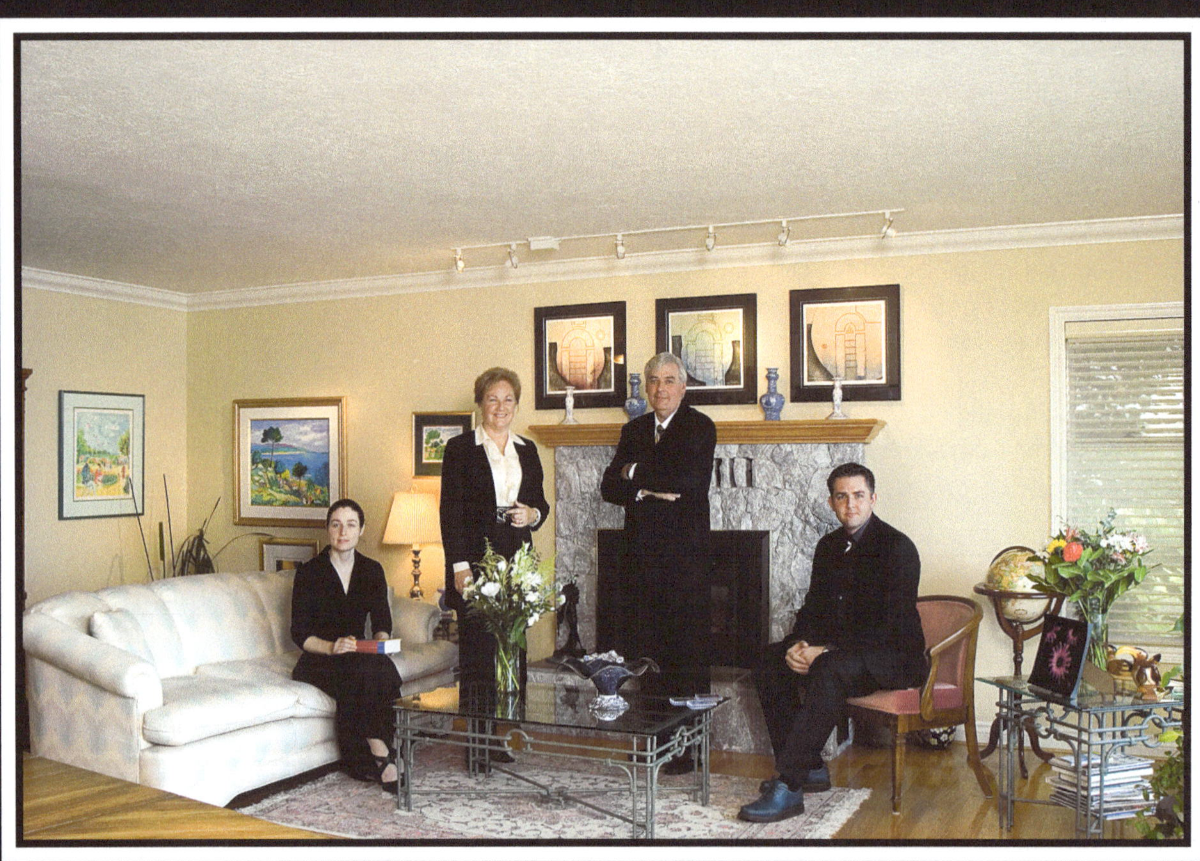

The Hoag Family

I am using their name because this is my sister Bev's family. I was fortunate when they invited me to photograph their family in their beautiful waterfront home. Just a short walk down to the water one may enjoy the refreshing ocean breezes. It is like a dream when I visit them and take advantage of this privilege.

It is important for me to share that I was paid in full even though I wanted to give them a break but it was not their wish. I think people, including relatives, should understand that photography is our profession and we have earned the right to be paid for our work and knowledge and understanding. Let's not water down our profession or cheapen the product because we will all suffer in the end.

Their house has a wonderful structure and design. I wanted to keep this formality and asked them to dress for the occasion. The placement speaks to me as part of their professions, social class and society in which they mingle. Our families are so attached; we visit and are so close, and have a loving bond in common.

There is so much I could say about my family that I love so much; their help and support in times of pain and suffering, may I return the favour in times of need, to practice the golden rule.

The symbol within this image is somewhat self explanatory, a strong pyramid, in everyone's body language and yet connected for the same reason. Art is displayed on the walls and over the fireplace. Wherever you go you will be influenced by the art in every room, and yet feel very comfortable somehow being lifted to a higher value of beauty.

I'll keep this short not because I have little to say but rather the opposite. I have so much I could say, an endless stream of stories and experiences we had together as a family. Travelling together to many parts of the world especially the birthday present they gave me when I was flown to Mexico, and the time I spent with them in Dubai when they worked and lived there.

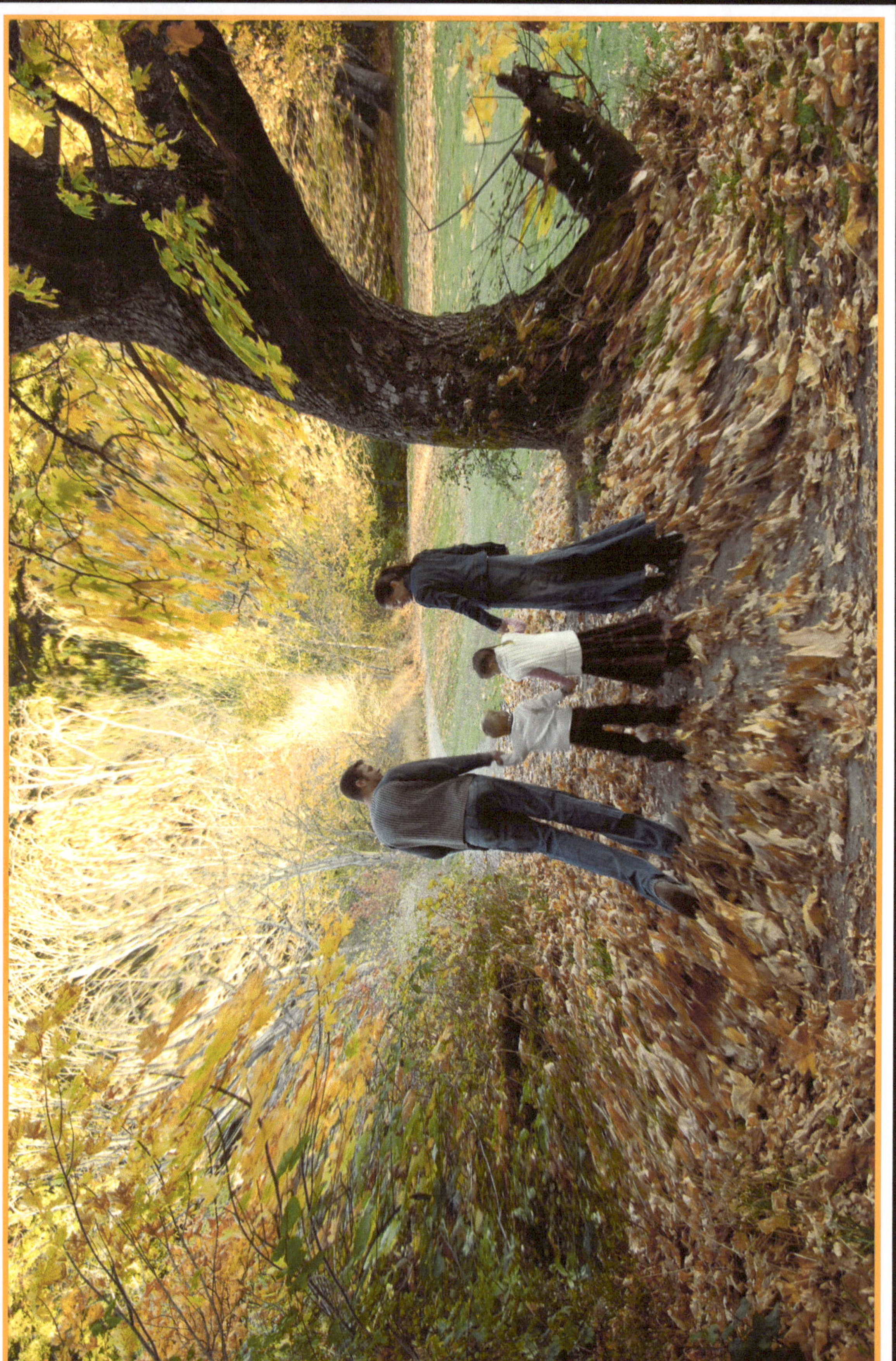

Halloween

I photographed this client's parents about ten years ago in Calgary, Alberta. To photograph them I used a grainy film and only a 35 mm camera but the results were intriguing. The image was mounted on a forty-inch canvas and hangs in their bedroom. Their son hired me to photograph his engagement. He said, "I like what you did for my parents!"

Since then I have photographed their wedding and used one of the images from their wedding in my first book which appears twice to illustrate two different principles of composition in photography. It is an image that was inspired by the groom when he said I like photographs with movement and action. I had him twirl his new bride and the dress gave the image a beautiful design.

When their first and second children were born they came back each time to have photographs taken. This past year they were interested in a family portrait walking together through the autumn leaves. I suggested photographing them from the back and adding a slight softness to the overall image. Since it was Halloween I felt it was appropriate to digitally enhance the outside edges of the image with a somewhat surrealistic and *spooky* effect.

What fun it is to photograph a client who becomes more than just a client. We develop a rapport, friendship and a trust in one another that allows us to appreciate each others' taste. The clients who we can work with repeatedly over the years make my profession enjoyable and worthwhile of a lifelong career. This is a blessing, love, excitement, challenge and privilege. How wonderful to have spent my working life in photography, with no retirement in sight because it is a labour of love. Nothing else I know of could be more appropriate for my personality and talent.

When they came to pick up their portraits I said, "I would love to give you a gift. What would you like?" Gifts are not offered very often but when they are I prefer giving added value. For instance a gift certificate that the client may wish to give to someone, perhaps a family member or friend, or they may even use it for themselves down the road. The gift we most often provide is a savings on frames. In this particular case the wife told me that they were expecting another baby, so I quickly suggested that my gift to them would be a professional service fee. Our professional service fee includes a consultation and the session, as well as a projection. I have mentioned this before but it doesn't hurt to be reminded that this sequence is so very important. By personally communicating with the client each time we are together I ensure that their needs and wants are clearly understood and fulfilled. This alleviates problems in the future and ensures their total satisfaction.

What a gift life can bless us with when we are guided by the Universe, something I refer to as the universal mind. To fulfill a dream still undreamt, a life of work yet unfinished or a life lived and yet not completed; may we be guided by a higher power, an unexplainable intuition not completely understood. To be driven, pulled, influenced and guided with a force from outside ourselves that is so great we cannot help but move forward, to do what we must do, what joy, what a blessing.

An Extraordinary Portrait

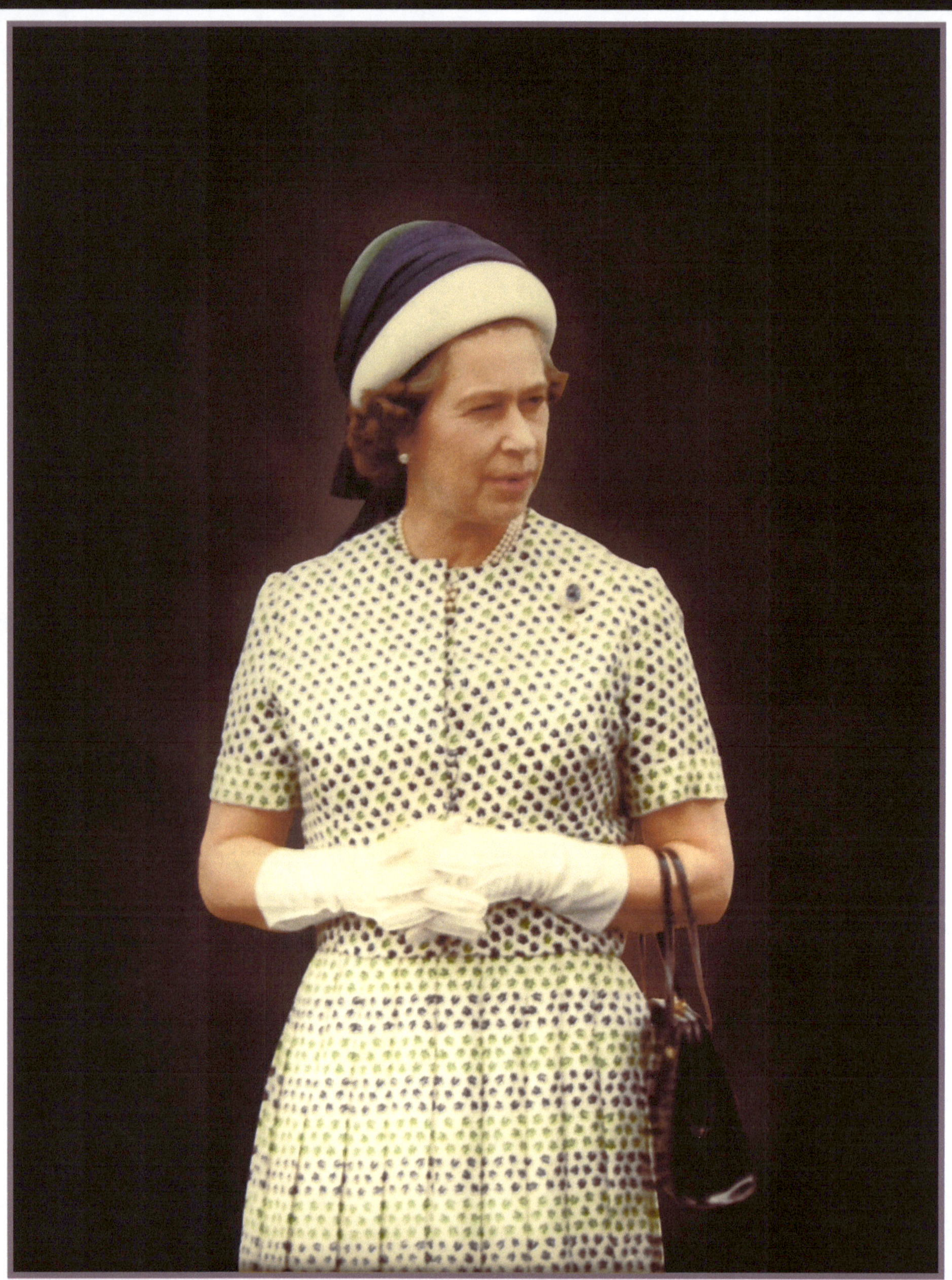

Her Majesty the Queen

Shortly after starting my business in Moose Jaw, Saskatchewan, I was commissioned by the city to photograph Queen Elizabeth II during her Royal Visit to Canada in 1978. Not only was it a great event for the city but equally an unspeakable experience for me. The protocol and the rehearsals we went through to prepare for her visit were quite extensive. I could spend pages explaining everything. For instance the distance to maintain between myself and the Queen, the location of the security guards along her route, the fact that I was not allowed to speak directly to the Queen or ask her to look a certain way and an endless list of other things that I could or could not do. Suffice to say that the Queen cannot be treated like an ordinary person. There are rules which must be followed and above all else, she cannot be told what to do, where to go or how to pose, at least not in an event such as this one.

It was a true privilege so early in my career but when you start from the top, so to speak, what is left? Well many years of photography followed with opportunity after privileged opportunity that have increased the value of my life as a photographer, a teacher and a writer but most of all as a father, a son, a brother and a human being. May we learn that our place in life is just that, our place. The experiences we have been privileged to explore and are granted in this life need to be cherished because karma is always around the corner. Our abundance in life will not only be measured in financial ways but I hope in goodness, selflessness and in ways that can't always be measured. In everything I do in my profession I am always feeling more deeply, doing more, caring more and loving more to become the person I was meant to be.

Life does have its rewards in spite of our ups and downs. Curves may come our way, unwanted as they may be, yet without our experiences who would we be? I dare not venture down that road of dreams, reality as we see it is our life, our purpose; may we be driven to the edge of our purpose so as to fulfill our destiny.

"You don't take a photograph.
You ask, quietly, to borrow it."
-Author Unknown

Self Portrait

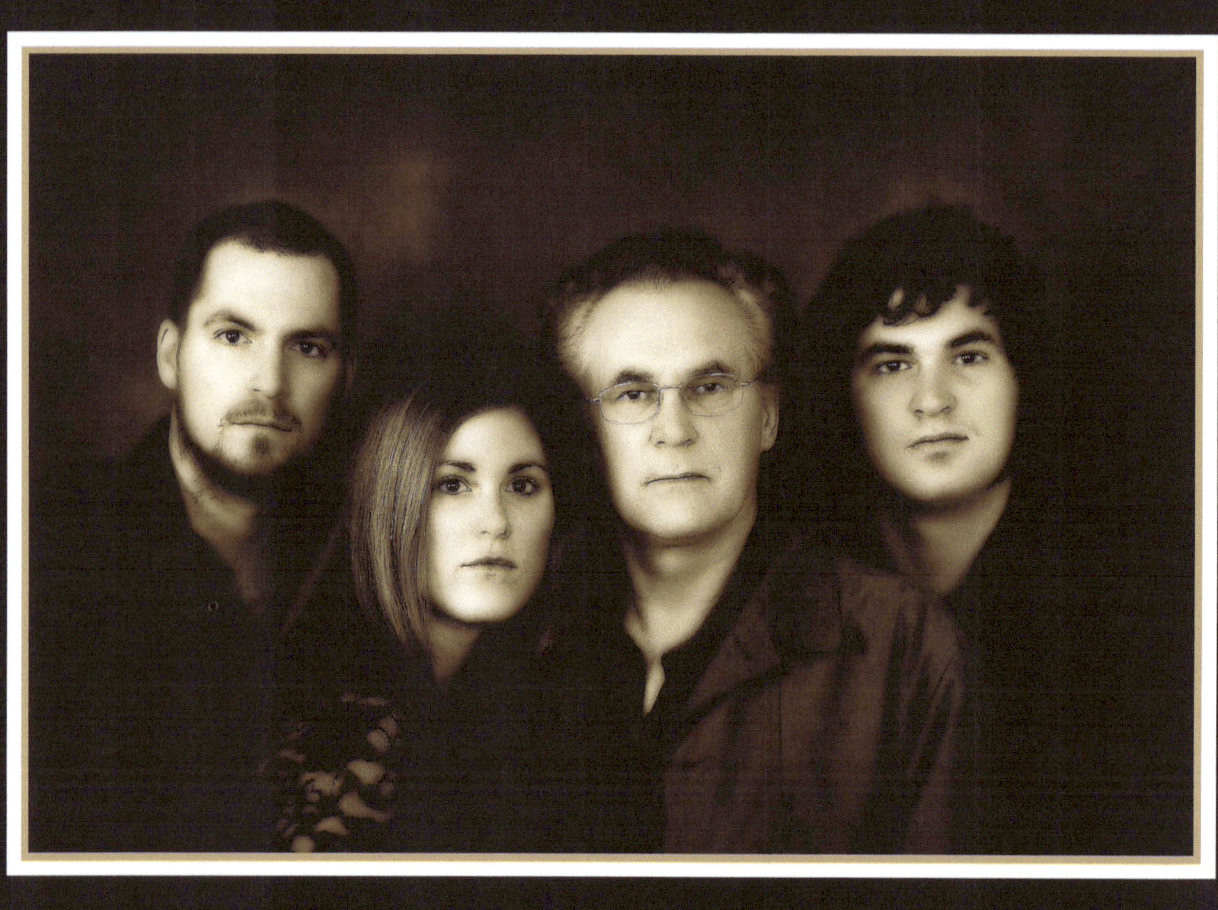

Myself, My Family

My three children are part of my flesh and blood and they are the most important people in my life. The hereafter may be a different story but I am so glad that I had these three blessings. What more could I hope for but to spend time with them and leave a legacy; to be remembered by my offspring and of course the many photographs I have taken. Writing will transcend my days on earth.

My family beyond my children, the larger family group so to speak has always been an important part to all of us. A family is not just by birth, it is also in our hearts. People are like a tapestry of lives, family histories woven together to give us a world of people bound by this great connection: father, mother, brother, sister and children. I once said, "Love is the muscle that can't be over worked in any relationship in all that we do and are." I had a father who has since passed away and a mother who has and still continues to exert a great deal of influence. My sister Bev has given me more than she can ever realize and in every way, her husband Gordon has adopted our family so whole heartedly and shared unselfishly in so many ways. Our children all want to be together, especially during holidays. What a treat it is to hear laughter and see the joy on their faces. My brother Brian worked so unselfishly at my studio for many years without complaint, working so hard as if it was his own and his wife Jean, a comedic, fun person and their one daughter, a family.

What family means to me may be very different to others and that is the way it should be. A family must be willing to share and enjoy each other's company; there should be a thrill and excitement, a love shared! Life's natural purpose is to propagate and fill this earth; I have had this privilege, to pass on my genes, making history within one's genealogy. This is the physical part but there are also the emotional parts which play a larger role in a family: loving, laughing, crying, feeling, helping and all that goes with it. Spirituality is our common belief system. It starts with a commonality in the beginning and then there are personal experiences that can add and/or change one's outlook, goals, hopes and values but in the end we are still bound by blood no matter what! May our love of humanity grow, our love for our family increase and our love of purpose shine forth with brilliance and radiance, creating an unspeakable joy filling us with glory.

Closing Remarks

Photography is a language on its own. To teach this language we must all be able to communicate on the same level. This has always been the challenge, no matter what universal language we choose.

There are those who can speak and others who can't see. We need to study everything in nature so we can begin to see as we do in art!

The *50 Principles of Composition in Photography* are similar to the ABC's of photography. Now as we explore beyond this elementary level we are working with words and perhaps sentences. I can teach only as much as someone can learn or as much as I am capable of communicating. As we learn language there are finer points such as pronunciation and enunciation that are embodied in the ability of the individual. The differences can be unique and pleasant or irritating depending on the listener if it is music or the viewer as in photography, as well as their culture and background. We sometimes use slang, short cuts or slur words together, as it were, like images that can be more readily understood in our part of the world. So much must be learned to satisfy our own comprehension.

Our approach needs to be global so that it can be understood by all people in every walk of life. To learn the language of art is a totally new endeavour. To learn the depth and breath and height is not enough. To learn the intuitive, to read between the lines, to be moved by our emotions, our hearts and even our anger, that is what we must all strive for in life.

Are we the observer or the creator or maybe even a critic? The observer has the simplest job, to interpret what they may want to feel at the time of viewing. The creator has to be driven, even passionately, to be able to express their ability. It all lies in the artist's ability, their vocabulary. Not so with the critic. Most often there is no cost, just their own ego, based on study and perhaps feeling the need to say something, anything, that may show their ability and judgment.

Let us learn to work together for a positive outcome in our beloved profession. What joy it must bring to all who can see and feel the benefit of even the simplest to the most profound creation. Photography has enabled human beings all over the world to communicate through photographs, perhaps somewhat similar to cave drawings, so as to preserve our history. May we be thankful and willing to share our memories and knowledge, for the future will soon be our past in this ever changing world!

About the Author

Klaus Bohn graduated from the Winona School of Professional Photography in 1972 and over the years has attended private classes from well known photographers who have lectured throughout the world including Joe Zeltsman, Monte Zucker, Linda Lapp-Murray, Donald Jack, Rocky Gunn, Yousuf Karsh, Arnold Newman, and many more.

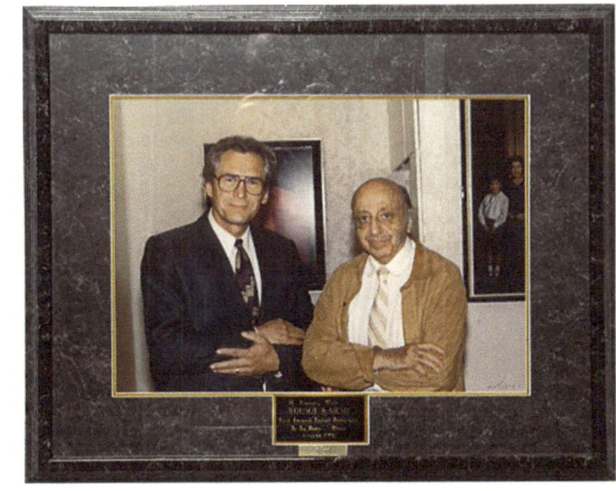

Klaus Bohn & Yousuf Karsh
Photo by Mitch Hippsley

Over the years he has worked to develop his unique style and received his Fellowship (F/SPPA) and Craftsman (CPA) in 1987 and his Masters of Photographic Arts (MPA) in 1989. He has also received his Accreditation in Child Photography (A) along with many other awards for Excellence in Photography.

He has been an active executive member of the Saskatchewan Professional Photographer's Association and held the title of Education Chairman as well as other positions. Klaus has also been a member of the Professional Photographers Association of British Columbia, Professional Photographers of Canada, the Professional Photographers of America and the Royal Society of Great Britain.

Klaus has taught professional photography since 1984 across Canada and the United States. Always trying to assist amateur and professional photographers alike, Klaus has also judged at many National and Regional photography competitions.

He has authored many magazine articles and has had his photos published in Range Finder Magazine, the Professional Photographers of Canada (PPOC) Magazine and others, as well as a series for Briar Patch Magazine.

Presently residing in Victoria, British Columbia, Klaus owns his own studio business, ***Photographic Art*** and completed his first book, *50 Principles of Composition in Photography*, in 2006. His current endeavours include writing and exploring new unique forms of photographic art. Klaus may be contacted directly through his Photographic Art web site: **www.photographicartvictoria.com**.

Index

www.ingramcontent.com/pod-product-compliance
Lightning Source LLC
LaVergne TN
LVHW070125110826
845147LV00002B/189

* 9 7 8 0 9 7 8 1 1 6 2 3 1 *